Educating Managers of Nonprofit Organizations

Educating Managers of Nonprofit Organizations

edited by
MICHAEL O'NEILL AND DENNIS R. YOUNG

with a Foreword by
PAUL YLVISAKER

PRAEGER

New York
Westport, Connecticut
London

Library of Congress Cataloging-in-Publication Data

Educating managers of nonprofit organizations.

  Bibliography: p.
  Includes index.
  1. Corporations, Nonprofit—Management—Study and
teaching (Higher)   2. Corporations, Nonprofit—
Management.   I. O'Neill, Michael.   II. Young, Dennis R.,
1943–
HD62.6.E38   1988   658'.048'071173   87–25869
ISBN 0–275–92609–5 (alk. paper)

Library of Congress Catalog Card Number: 87–25869

ISBN: 0–275–92609–5

First published in 1988

Praeger Publishers, One Madison Avenue, New York, NY 10010
An imprint of Greenwood Publishing Group, Inc.

Printed in the United States of America

∞

The paper used in this book complies with the
Permanent Paper Standard issued by the National
Information Standards Organization (Z39.48–1984).

10 9 8 7 6 5 4 3 2

Terry Walker McAdam

Executive Vice President and Program Director of the Conrad N. Hilton Foundation, Terry McAdam, was one of the pioneers of the nonprofit management field. Terry played a major role in the inauguration of education and training programs for nonprofit managers through his work at the Hilton Foundation and earlier at New York Community Trust; through his assistance in the development of new programs at Columbia University, the University of Colorado, Case Western Reserve University, the University of San Francisco, and elsewhere; through his teaching at Fordham University, the New School for Social Research, New York University, and the University of San Francisco; through his prolific writing and speaking; and through his doctoral research at New York University. Before his tragic death on September 26, 1986, Terry had prepared the first draft of the chapter that appears in this book as coauthored by him and Robert Leduc. In some small recognition of all that he contributed to the field of nonprofit management education, we dedicate this book to the memory of Terry McAdam.

Contents

Foreword

This collection of essays raises more questions than it answers. But simply by confronting issues that have never been systematically addressed before, this volume is assured the status of a landmark study.

Its topic is the training of managers for the nonprofit sector. Until a decade ago, the myriads of nonprofit organizations—from the Red Cross to the tiniest of neighborhood associations that dot the American countryside and give the nation so much of its character—had never been thought of as a sector. It took the Filer Commission on Private Philanthropy and Public Needs to see and label it as such: a universe of its own, distinguishable in its aggregate from government on the one side and business on the other. The abstraction identified by the Filer Commission took concrete form with the establishment soon after of the Independent Sector, an umbrella agency that expressed the collectivity of the sector's interests and took on the responsibility of stating and defending them.

Those two happenings simply galvanized a consciousness that in the words and realities of the Sixties was "blowing in the winds". An explosion in the numbers and prominence of private bodies serving the public interest converted what had long been taken for granted into the dawning awareness of a precious element of American society.

It was evident how aware and how precious both became during the shift from affluence to scarcity that startled the nation into budgetary cutbacks beginning in the late seventies. Burgeoning social need was heaped on diminishing resources; there had been no option for all three sectors except to maximize the efficiency and effectiveness of their operations.

Inevitably, the world of the nonprofits and those who support them has become explicitly and centrally concerned with the quality of management. Not simply agency by agency, function by function, specialty by specialty. But generically: How do we recruit, train, and continuously develop the level of competence and sophistication required to make the entire constellation of nonprofit organizations an effective and efficient instrument of American society?

Honor this group of authors for collectively recognizing a generic challenge, for elevating a congeries of particularistic concerns to the level where the question of managerial competence has long been handled with respect to business and government. It is commentary in itself that campuses across this country have for decades been the homes of schools, of businesses and of government; nowhere can one find an equivalent school generically concerned with the nonprofits.

It is too early to prescribe how best such generic concerns should be catalogued and structured on an academic campus (indeed, to what extent the function should become the preserve of the University). But it is by no means too early to raise the host of questions that have to be answered if viable programs of training for nonprofit management are to be developed. This group of essayists is united in their agreement that such programs are needed. But they unblinkingly raise the formidable questions that demand satisfactory answers. To their credit, too, they understand that satisfactory answers will not appear from sudden insight or pontifical assertions. What is called for, they agree, is thoughtful experimentation and the gradual evolution of "best practice." The chronicle of future programs of management training for the nonprofits will undoubtedly follow the kind of evolutionary development that has arduously been worked out for business and public administration. But hopefully, given the urgency of the need, that history will be accelerated and abbreviated.

By collecting under one cover the questions that have to be addressed, and in the richness of the insights and suggestions provided, these authors will help immeasurably to speed and enlighten that evolution. They have made a singular and pioneering contribution.

Paul Ylvisaker
Charles William Eliot
Professor of Education
Harvard University

Acknowledgment

We wish to thank the Alfred P. Sloan Foundation for support of the conference on Educating Managers of Nonprofit Organizations upon which this book is based.

Educating Managers of Nonprofit Organizations

1

Educating Managers of Nonprofit Organizations

Michael O'Neill and Dennis R. Young

During the last decade, and particularly within the last five years, considerable attention has been given to the management of private nonprofit organizations and to the question of how managers of these organizations should be educated or trained. Historically, these managers learned administration almost solely through on-the-job experience, sometimes supplemented by in-service training. A few nonprofit professionals enrolled in the administration tracks of discipline-based degree programs in social work, health care, arts, education, and religion. Generic management programs such as business and public administration largely ignored the nonprofit sector, occasional catalogue rhetoric notwithstanding. However, recent years have seen the growth of a new industry of management training and consulting services for nonprofit organizations, as well as the development of university degree and certificate programs for nonprofit managers, as documented in *An Independent Sector Resource Directory of Education and Training Opportunities and Other Services* (Gray 1987).

This new effort is potentially of great importance. The nonprofit sector constitutes a significant part of the overall American economy, some 5 to 10 percent of all economic activity by various measures (Hodgkinson and Weitzman 1986). The sector employs as many civilians as the federal government and fifty state governments combined. A recent Urban Institute study showed that in some metropolitan areas, the nonprofit sector is significantly larger than local government (Lippert, Gutowski, and Salamon 1984). Furthermore, the nonprofit sector has grown faster than either business or government in recent decades (Rudney and Weitzman 1984). The size, complexity, and uniqueness of the private nonprofit sector make management development for the sector an important educational issue.

A critical question in this educational arena is whether the nonprofit sector is in some sense a coherent entity, as the business and government sectors are thought to be, thereby permitting a generic approach to the education of nonprofit managers. The nonprofit sector possesses great internal diversity, though this is also true of business and government. Whether the diversity of nonprofits is so great as to render unwise a generic approach to management education is a central issue here. But for practical reasons alone the diversity of nonprofits argues for increased attention to the educational question: the nonprofit sector contains organizations not only in the arts, education, health care, social work, and religion—the few nonprofit-related disciplines whose schools pay serious attention to administration—but also in a myriad of other fields such as advocacy, research, community development, trade associations, and foundations. The fact that such organizations fall not only outside the business and government sectors but also outside the "mainline" nonprofit disciplines appears to argue for a more comprehensive approach to nonprofit management education.

Added to these considerations of sector size and diversity is the fact that nonprofit organizations have experienced major changes and environmental pressures in the last two decades, a situation that has made management a crucial factor in the survival and effectiveness of these organizations. Much of the turmoil has centered on the phenomenon of government funding. The rapid growth of the nonprofit sector in the 1960s and 1970s was due in no small part to the infusion of federal funds into the social and health services, arts, education, research, and other fields where nonprofits play a major role. In addition to expanding its own programs, government often provided these services through contracts with nonprofits (Kramer 1985a). Consequently, the nonprofit sector required entrepreneurial managers who could take advantage of these new opportunities and guide organizations through periods of rapid growth. But in the 1980s the picture changed dramatically. The Reagan administration not only imposed severe budgetary cutbacks but also created new expectations that the private sector, including the "voluntary" sector, would and should fill the gap left by the withdrawal of the federal government (Salamon and Abramson 1982). Nonprofits went from the years of plenty to the years of scarcity and survival, and thus needed managers who could run a tight ship while developing new funding sources through more sophisticated marketing and fundraising and through for-profit ventures (Skloot 1987).

These developments led the authors to approach the Alfred P. Sloan Foundation for support of a conference and publication on this topic. The Sloan Foundation, long active in management education efforts, generously responded with a grant. Praeger agreed to publish the revised papers of the conference as a book.

The conference, held at the University of San Francisco in November 1986, included ten papers presented to fifty invited participants, the latter representing academics, funders, technical assistance providers, and others who had played a leading role in the development of university-based programs for nonprofit managers. A complete list of speakers and participants is found in the Appendix. About two months prior to the conference, the draft papers were mailed to conference participants, who were asked to read them and send back written comments prior to the conference. At the conference itself, the papers were discussed in small- and large-group settings, and written summaries of these discussions were provided. Following the conference, the authors revised their papers in the light of written and oral comments received.

The following sections of this introductory chapter delineate (a) the principal differences between nonprofits and other organizations and the implications of these differences for nonprofit management education, (b) the key issues that emerged in preparation for and during the conference, and (c) the major conclusions of the papers and the conference. Although we have tried to distill the principal themes of the papers and the conference discussions, inevitably we cannot do full justice to either.

CHARACTERISTICS OF NONPROFITS VS. OTHER ORGANIZATIONS

The aim of this section is to describe the characteristics of nonprofit organizations that differentiate them from business or government organizations, as well as the dimensions along which nonprofit organizations differ significantly among themselves. Having done this, we then ask what these characteristics may imply for nonprofit management and nonprofit management education.

The discussion is divided into four parts focusing on (1) distinctive management-related features held in common by nonprofit organizations, (2) internal variety in the functions of management within nonprofit organizations, (3) the diversity among organizations in the nonprofit sector, and (4) the interdependence between nonprofits and organizations in other sectors.

In brief, we suggest that nonprofits are distinctive in:

- The ambiguity of their performance criteria and the complexity of their management-related values.
- The legal and financial constraints under which they operate.
- Some of the sources from which they derive economic sustenance.
- The kinds of personnel they employ.
- Their governance structures.

Moreover, we observe that nonprofits employ two different kinds of managers—managers of programs and managers of organizational business functions—and that the two may not necessarily require the same kinds of education and background.

In addition, we note that there is considerable diversity in the population of nonprofit organizations in terms of:

• General purpose, e.g., mutual versus public benefit orientation.
• Fields of service.
• Size.

Finally, we observe that nonprofits are highly interdependent with government and business.

Each of these features of nonprofit organizations is argued to have important implications for nonprofit management and the education of nonprofit managers.

Distinctive Features of Nonprofits

Values. Nominally at least, organizations in the business and government sectors are guided by relatively clear performance criteria. In the business sector, the objective is to make a profit. For government agencies, the objective is to carry out programs as defined by elected officials whose views presumably reflect the will of their constituents. Certainly, organizations in these sectors often stray far from the mark in meeting these objectives, but there is general agreement that these goals represent appropriate frames of reference from which to judge effectiveness.

The nonprofit sector is fundamentally different. Like business, nonprofit organizations are required to break even financially; and, like government, nonprofit organizations are mandated by their charters, legal status, and tax benefits to act in the public interest or in the interest of some defined constituency. But these guidelines are more in the nature of broad constraints than specific goals or objectives. In fact, nonprofit organizations have to decide for themselves what they should be doing and how it will be determined whether or not they are doing it well.

One way to understand the difference between nonprofits and organizations in other sectors is to realize that the particular activities that business and government organizations undertake are *instrumental* to achieving their overall objectives. For nonprofits, the particular service or the given constituency or the articulated cause is of *primary* concern, not subservient to an overriding financial or political bottom line.

The management implications of this special character of nonprofit organizations are not completely clear, but that character does suggest that nonprofit managers need special skills and shoulder unusual responsibilities.

These nonprofit managers must be able to determine and articulate what their organizations should be doing and then work with others to implement those goals. This requirement appears to have both practical and philosophic aspects to it. Practically speaking, nonprofit managers need, on the one hand, the planning skills to understand the environments in which their organizations are enmeshed, the alternative courses of action they could take, and the implications of those actions. On the other hand, they need the "people" skills with which to deal effectively with staff, volunteers, clients, and supporters. Even more important, the nonprofit manager needs some philosophic basis on which to set the course. What is it that is worth doing? How ought that to be done? What is the proper place of efficiency versus other values such as equity and participation? Answers to these questions require not only insight into a particular organization's mission but also some understanding of charity and the philanthropic tradition, concepts of social welfare, and basic tenets of ethics and morality. Similar issues arise in managing government and business organizations, but the status of nonprofits appears to warrant special attention to the value basis of managerial decision-making.

Hence, one may inquire, is a new form of education needed for nonprofit managers, one that centers on the pressing value-related issues faced by these individuals? Or can such value concerns be just as effectively addressed in a management school that serves other sectors of the society? And, more concretely, what are the subject matter and methodological training that can best prepare nonprofit managers to cope with these fundamental considerations of values and direction-setting for their organizations?

Practical Differences. We have already alluded to one important practical difference between nonprofit organizations and organizations in other sectors—the lack of a clear bottom line. There are other practical dimensions along which the nonprofit sector is distinctive. These include the legal constraints on nonprofit organizations, the ways in which nonprofits derive their revenues, the structure and composition of the nonprofit workforce, and the relationship between the nonprofit organization and its governing board.

Depending on their particular Internal Revenue Service (IRS) classification, nonprofit organizations may be legally constrained in the degree of their political activity, their ability to raise funds through deductible contributions, and the necessity to pay taxes of various kinds. But all nonprofit organizations have in common the so-called nondistribution constraint. Indeed, this constraint, which prohibits a nonprofit organization from distributing financial surpluses to directors, staff, or members of the organization, is commonly cited as the defining characteristic of a nonprofit organization (Hansmann 1980).

The nondistribution constraint has wide-ranging practical and ethical implications for nonprofit organizations, implications that seem to call for a unique managerial perspective. It raises the basic question, how much explicit surplus should be declared by an organization and how much should be avoided by fine-tuning salaries and other expenditures so that they match actual revenues? What are the efficiency implications of the latter approach? What are the pros and cons of showing a deficit? For example, do deficits encourage higher levels of giving from philanthropic sources, or are they a sign of poor management? What are the uses to which financial surpluses should be put? Should the organization attempt to build up an endowment through surplus accumulation? All these difficult questions are raised by the nondistribution constraint.

Moreover, the constraint raises certain personnel incentive issues (Young 1984). If profit-sharing cannot be used, what other motivational techniques can or should govern the compensation of nonprofit employees? And how closely can "merit" raises be tied to the financial well-being of the organization?

The sources from which nonprofit organizations derive their revenues would also appear to create unique managerial problems. Nonprofits are widely divergent as to funding sources. Some nonprofits, like schools, colleges, and arts organizations, depend heavily on revenues derived from the marketplace, i.e., fees and charges. Others, like religious and many human service organizations, rely mostly on individual and institutional gifts. Hansmann (1980) gives the name "donative nonprofits" to those organizations that depend primarily on grants and philanthropy. Still others, such as community development organizations, research organizations, and most health care and social service agencies, derive their principal income directly or indirectly from government funds. In fact, Salamon (1985) argues that philanthropy now accounts for a relatively small proportion of nonprofit revenues and that the most important source of funds is government— either through grant or contract funding or third-party financing arrangements such as Medicaid and Medicare. Finally, some nonprofits, such as foundations, are supported primarily by endowments. Many nonprofits receive funds from several or all of the above sources.

The basic point is that nonprofits are unique both in the fact that their sources of revenue are widely mixed (both within and among organizations) and in the fact that most nonprofits depend significantly on nonmarket sources of funds—philanthropy and government. Thus, nonprofit managers are required to have a variety of resource development skills, ranging from marketing skills for developing commercial revenues to political and interpersonal skills for obtaining funds from government, foundations, corporations, and private benefactors. No other sector seems to put such diverse demands on managers to maintain organizational sources of sustenance and growth.

The political and interpersonal skills required of nonprofit managers apply to more than just the domain of fundraising. Nonprofit organizations are also qualitatively different in the types of personnel involved. At the staff level, government and business work is largely carried out by paid employees who report to superiors through clearly defined lines of authority. In most nonprofit organizations, however, the situation is much more complex. As Cecily Selby (1978) has written, nonprofits often consist of three parallel hierarchies—those for paid staff, volunteers, and professionals. Aside from the fact that these three groups must be coordinated with one another, each group poses its own special managerial problems. The management of paid nonprofit staff most closely resembles personnel management in the other sectors, though even for this group the mix of staff motivations may be substantially different (Mirvis and Hackett 1983) from the mix in other sectors. But the more significant differences in personnel between nonprofits and other kinds of organizations pertain to professionals and volunteers. Majone (1980) and others have cited nonprofit organizations as the natural locus for professional staff. Nonprofits are seen to provide the necessary service orientation, quality concerns, and degree of employee discretion and autonomy to allow professionals—in education, health care, social work, the arts, and so on—to pursue their crafts. Thus, professionals in these fields tend to be concentrated in the nonprofit sector.

Even more than professionals, volunteers gravitate to the nonprofit sector. Not surprisingly, recent reports on dimensions of the independent sector by Hodgkinson and Weitzman (1984, 1986) demonstrate that volunteer effort is overwhelmingly concentrated in nonprofit organizations as compared to business or government.

What are the managerial implications of the uniquely different personnel compositions of nonprofit organizations? It is clear that since nonprofits depend greatly on the efforts of professionals and volunteers, nonprofit managers must be especially sensitive to the particular needs of these groups—needs that may include flexible scheduling of work for volunteers, finding nonpecuniary ways to reward volunteers, providing sufficient room for discretion and growth by professionals, and providing recognition for professional achievements. Perhaps even more important, the nonprofit manager must recognize that volunteers and professionals, to a substantial degree, march to different drummers than do other, paid, staff. Both groups may come to the organization with their own agendas, agendas that may diverge from that of the organization's management. And both groups may have external reference groups to whom they respond and gear their efforts. Professionals are especially likely to play to the gallery of their peers in the professions and be judged and rewarded by professional achievements as much as organizational contributions per se.

A fourth area of practical difference between nonprofits and other organizations is that of organizational governance. There are some who argue that the processes of organizational governance are substantially the same from sector to sector (Dayton 1985). After all, businesses have boards of directors and government agencies have legislative and advisory committees to whom the organizations' chief executive officers report. But there are manifold differences as well. Some of these differences are technical, such as whether the chief executive has a vote on the board (usually not in nonprofits) and what particular controls and responsibilities are allocated to the board versus the staff. Other differences include whether directors are paid (again, nonprofit directors usually are not) and whether new board members have adequate preparation or background for their board responsibilities (in nonprofits they often do not).

Still other differences are more fundamental. The relationship between the board of trustees and the chief executive officer is thought to be more treacherous in a nonprofit organization than in other kinds of organizations, perhaps because of ambiguities and misunderstandings that easily arise in the nonprofit context. Again due to the absence of clear bottom-line performance measures, the board's policy-making, supportive, and fiduciary roles are crucial in a nonprofit organization. Ironically, the management of nonprofit boards is often so problematic because these boards are so organizationally important. Indeed, it has been recognized that management of the board requires special training and materials geared to this sector alone (O'Connell 1985).

In summary, the legal constraints, revenue sources, types of personnel, and nature of governance appear to create substantial practical differences in managing nonprofits versus managing other kinds of organizations. But are these differences sufficient to require a substantially separate approach to educating nonprofit managers? And, in whatever context nonprofit managers might be trained, what are the crucial skills and areas of knowledge they must master in order to cope with these practical aspects of organizational management?

Intra-organizational Variation

There are several different kinds of managers. For example, in a reasonably large organization there may be top managers, middle-level managers, and lower-level administrators and supervisors. Moreover, managers oversee different types of organizational activity. Some are responsible for the production or delivery of client services. For example, in a university, there are deans and department heads managing the production and delivery of instructional services in a variety of disciplines. In a social agency, there may be administrators for counseling services, institutional services, medical services, educational services, children's services, and so on. Managers of this kind may be labeled "program managers." Obviously, the particular kinds of program managers an agency employs vary with the field of service in which that agency is engaged.

Agencies also employ other kinds of managers who are responsible for the operational side of organizational activities. These "business managers" may be in charge of finances, physical plant, purchasing, payroll and personnel, support services, public relations, marketing, and the like. In many organizations, business and program managers are clearly differentiated. In other organizations, some managerial positions, particularly at the top levels, combine business and program responsibilities. For example, some arts organizations have both artistic and administrative directors, while other arts organizations have a single top executive who is responsible for both functions.

Despite the partial overlap of business and program responsibilities, the distinction between the two raises important questions about the appropriate training for nonprofit managers. Presumably, program-type managers need to be well grounded in the professional disciplines in which they work—education, health care, social work, the arts, and so on. But such is not clearly the case for business-type managers, although most people would argue that some disciplinary background is useful. (There is a parallel here with the literature on business organizations, where it is argued that one problem of modern American business is that managers are unfamiliar with the nature of the product and the character of the work on the shop floor. See, for example, Peters and Waterman 1982.) Does the distinction between business and program managers imply that there should be two different modes of nonprofit management education? Should generic nonprofit managers—unspecialized by professional service area—be educated for the operational side of nonprofits, while program managers are developed for those on the service delivery side? Would such a two-pronged approach satisfy those in the nonprofit sector who say that managing a nonprofit organization in whatever capacity requires having the appropriate professional experience as a prerequisite? Or must the field of nonprofit management education forever confine itself to providing management training to experienced professionals who have found their way into nonprofit management, sometimes serendipitously? Can universities, instead, begin to train individuals who view nonprofit management as a career from the start? More radically, is it possible to educate nonprofit managers, even program managers, from scratch by providing professional courses and field experiences within a graduate management curriculum? Clearly, answers to these questions will shape the future of nonprofit management education.

Interorganization Variation

Thus far we have discussed a number of management-related factors that appear to differentiate nonprofits as a group from other kinds of organizations, and we have considered the variety of managerial contexts within nonprofit organizations. It remains to ask what the diversity among nonprofit organizations implies for nonprofit management and the education of nonprofit managers.

As suggested above, the population of nonprofit organizations is highly diverse, and one argument for developing the field of nonprofit management education is to cover the gaps left by the professional schools in those few professional areas that address this subject. The variety of nonprofit organizations manifests itself along a number of different lines. In general terms, there are at least two basic kinds of nonprofit organizations: philanthropic, public-service–oriented nonprofits whose purpose is to serve segments of the public at large, and mutual benefit organizations such as clubs, professional and trade associations, mutual insurance companies, and unions, whose purpose is to serve the needs of their own members. Within these broad categories there are further divisions, e.g., between public service organizations that are charitable, donations to which may be deducted from income taxes, and advocacy organizations to which such giving may not be deductible. Finally, churches form a subcategory by themselves, being tax–exempt and eligible to receive deductible contributions, though not having to file for charitable status with the IRS, and engaging in services both for their own members and for segments of society at large.

In addition, we have referred previously to the differences among nonprofit organizations in terms of their sources of revenue, i.e., the distinction between "donative" and "commercial" nonprofits and organizations with substantial mixes of revenues from sales of services and from grants, contributions, and governmental budget allocations. Another category of nonprofits may be termed "fiscal intermediaries," i.e., organizations such as foundations, United Ways, third–party insurers, and the like, which gather funds from one set of sources (government, individual donors, institutional donors, subscribers) and distribute them to direct-service organizations.

Nonprofit organizations are also highly differentiated by fields of service. As measured by employment, revenues, or expenditures, health services constitute the largest segment, followed by education and research; religious organizations; social services; civic, social, and fraternal organizations; arts and culture; and others (Hodgkinson and Weitzman 1984, 1986).

Finally, nonprofit organizations vary considerably by size, and differences in size are also associated with the field of service in which an organization is engaged. For example, while nonprofit hospitals and universities tend to be large, having budgets in the tens of millions, other human service organizations (including those in health, education, social service, advocacy, and arts and culture, but excluding hospitals and institutions of higher education) are mostly small. Indeed, Disney, Kimmich, and Musselwhite (1984) found that only 15 percent of such organizations in a national sample had annual budgets of over a million dollars in 1982, while 47 percent had expenditures of under $100,000 per year.

The considerable heterogeneity among nonprofit organizations raises a number of important issues for management and managerial education. One question, of course, is whether divisions within the sector are so deep as to preclude a common approach to managerial education. For example, are the differences between social services and arts and cultural nonprofits so vast as to require separate management training, or is there enough in common in the basic operations and structure of such nonprofit organizations to allow a unified approach? This question is an obvious one because there already exist graduate school programs in art, social service, health, education, and religious administration. But the other lines of division within the nonprofit sector suggest similar questions. Do managers of public benefit versus mutual benefit organizations require different training? Do managers of market-oriented nonprofits require an education that differs from that of managers for grant-oriented organizations? And so on.

Perhaps the most provocative question along these lines pertains to the size-related diversity of nonprofits. One can logically ask not only whether there might be more in common between large nonprofits and large businesses or government agencies than between large and small nonprofits, or more in common between small businesses and small nonprofits than between small and large nonprofits. Indeed, this line of questioning leads one to ask whether there should be separate management education programs for small and large organizations, differentiated not by sector but by size.

It is also interesting to ask whether this same question arises with respect to management education in other sectors. The answer seems to be "yes and no." In public administration, the issue seems less salient, as government agencies are generally large or, at the least, small public sector agencies are usually embedded within larger-scale bureaucratic structures. In the business sector, however, this is a major issue. Indeed, business schools have been criticized considerably for their inordinate attention to large corporations and their relative neglect of small business and entrepreneurial activity (Young 1985).

In short, there is no such thing as the prototypical nonprofit organization, though the same might be said of business and government agencies as well. Thus, a key question in the development of nonprofit management education is whether, as has apparently been decided in the other sectors, nonprofits have enough in common to justify and encourage a distinct, unitary management education tradition of their own.

Sector Interdependence

Related to the issue of sector diversity is the observation that none of the sectors, least of all the nonprofit sector, is isolated from the others. Indeed, the operations of business, government, and nonprofit organizations are highly intertwined. Lester Salamon (1985), for example, has described the delivery of public services in this country as a system of "third-party government," by which he means that a major portion of government expenditure is funneled through nonprofit organizations for the purpose of service delivery. Conversely, the largest portion of the revenue of nonprofit organizations derives from government. Similarly, we can observe that nonprofit organizations are governed by trustees, many of whom are business people, and that corporate contributions and commercial revenues are a small but increasingly important part of nonprofit funding.

These patterns of interconnection raise a number of management-training–related issues. First, they seem to suggest that no matter where nonprofit managers are educated they need to know much about business and government as well as their own sector. And if similar observations of interdependence apply to the other sectors, then it suggests that perhaps managers from all sectors ought to be educated under the same roof. Finally, the pattern of interdependence raises the issue of career scenarios for nonprofit managers. In particular, do the patterns of interdependence suggest that nonprofit managers do or should work in two or three sectors over the course of their careers rather than in the nonprofit sector alone? And, if so, how are such sector-switching managers appropriately prepared for such careers?

The foregoing discussion of the character of the nonprofit sector—what management-related characteristics these organizations have in common, how management responsibilities vary within nonprofit organizations, how nonprofit organizations vary from one another, and how nonprofits are interdependent with business and government—has raised a number of important issues bearing on how nonprofit managers should be educated. In the following section, we summarize the principal points made relative to these issues by the speakers and the participants at the conference.

PRINCIPAL ISSUES IN THE EDUCATION OF NONPROFIT MANAGERS

Need for Nonprofit Management Education

Although the conference was called to analyze the emergence of such programs and included many of the nation's leaders in this movement, one of the important questions raised was the rationale for nonprofit management programs. The actual practice of recent decades might suggest that there is no such need. One might argue that, after all, "management is management," and that the best thing a nonprofit leader could do would be to enroll in an MBA or MPA program. A variation on this theme is the idea that although there are some organizational and management differences between nonprofits and business or government agencies, the differences are much less important than the commonalities, and therefore a generic management program for all sectors is the most effective route.

Alternatively, one might hold that since most nonprofits deal with well-established disciplines (religion, education, health care, social work, arts and culture, etc.) management training should be closely related to the discipline and therefore offered through such programs as arts administration, pastoral ministry, educational administration, and the Master of Social Work degree. Finally, one might contend that since the great majority of nonprofits are either very small or volunteer-based, full-scale graduate programs for nonprofit managers are not necessary.

The rationale for generic nonprofit management education programs is discussed in several of the following chapters. Simon Slavin, Founding Dean Emeritus of Temple University's School of Social Administration, argues that the professions—social work, medicine, education, the arts—have dominated the culture of nonprofit organizations and therefore that these organizations cannot be effectively managed by those inexperienced in the profession, since professionals do not easily tolerate being directed by those outside their disciplines. Moreover, those untrained in the profession will not be technically able to judge the performance of professional employees, yet this evaluative function cannot be delegated without serious damage to the appearance of administrative competence. Slavin also argues that the clinical professions are substantially different from one another in culture, language, and protocols, so that it is not practical to educate generic managers on the theory that they could cross from one professional area to another.

Paul DiMaggio, Professor of Sociology and Executive Director of the Program on Non-Profit Organizations at Yale University, argues for a different view based on content analysis of managerial jobs in different kinds of nonprofit organizations. DiMaggio suggests that if required skills were uniformly distributed among alternative managerial jobs in the nonprofit sector, then a generic management curriculum would be efficient. Alternatively, if certain skills applied only to a certain set of jobs, and other skills applied only to other jobs, then two or more specialized management education programs would be needed. Between these extremes lie various possibilities for core skills applying to all jobs plus specialized skills applying to subsets of jobs. Such patterns would call for a core curriculum with various specializations appended. Thus, the preferred education program for nonprofit managers is an empirical matter that should derive from detailed study of what these managers actually do. In a similarly empirical vein, DiMaggio also argues that the current emergence of nonprofit management programs in universities represents an important social innovation that could be studied for what it reveals about nonprofit management. If many different program varieties are winnowed down over time to just a few different models, as has occurred in the business administration and public administration fields, this would suggest some conclusions about the educational needs of nonprofit organization managers.

Finally, Reynold Levy, President of the AT&T Foundation, argues against relegating nonprofit management to existing professional schools and for the emergence of this field as something unto itself within the university setting. Levy notes that the clinical professional schools do not typically teach management, at most occasionally layering management on top of an already full curriculum. In this context, management is much less important than the profession and is therefore neglected.

Values Related to Nonprofit Management Education

Legal scholars, economists, sociologists, and philosophers continue to clarify the nature of private nonprofit organizations and the way in which they differ from for-profit or government organizations. This clarification process is far from complete, but it does seem that one of the important ways in which nonprofits differ from business or government enterprises lies in the value orientation of nonprofits. It is therefore not surprising that the values question emerged as a major issue related to nonprofit management education programs. Much of the conference discussion revolved around the question of values. If the nonprofit sector is distinct from business or government, what are the special values that distinguish this sector from the others? Presumably those values would have significant impact on curricula for nonprofit management programs, if, as suggested by Chester Barnard (1938) and many others, executives must be able to articulate and even symbolize the values and visions of their organizations.

Two major competing values emerged in the discussion. One school of thought was that *pluralism*, the freedom to pursue any of a wide variety of causes and beliefs, was the principal distinguishing value of the nonprofit sector. Nonprofit organizations can pursue activities which are neither profitable in the marketplace nor supportable by a governing coalition in the public sector. All that is required is that some constituency be found that will support the organization's chosen mission.

A second school of thought was that nonprofit organizations exist to *benefit the public* and that it is for this purpose that tax exemption and other forms of special treatment are granted to nonprofits by law.

A tension arises between these two schools in the case of nonprofit organizations whose missions entail opposite conceptions of the public interest, for example, organizations working for and against gun control. If pluralism is the key value, there is no problem in justifying this diversity. But if public interest is also a key value, as most agree it is, then how can the underlying value structure of nonprofit organizations be codified and taught? Brian O'Connell, President of Independent Sector, suggests that pluralism is the primary value of the nonprofit world, with the understanding that organizations intended explicitly to promote harm must be rejected. Under this criterion, the Ku Klux Klan and various neo-Nazi groups presumably would not qualify as legitimate members of the nonprofit sector, though both the National Rifle Association and pro–gun-control groups presumably would. Others at the conference argued that the public interest is primary and that the dilemma is resolved by the view that nonprofit organizations may pursue opposing policies so long as they sincerely intend, and have legitimate grounds to argue that, their policies are designed to promote public welfare.

A related value question is, how should nonprofit managers weigh organizational survival and responsiveness to funders against the values of independence, autonomy, creativity, and innovation? Are nonprofits simply vehicles by which funders (e.g., government, foundations, individuals) carry out various public purposes, or are they autonomous institutions part of whose role is to help define the public purpose, such as how and what should be done for various minorities, constituencies, and interest groups? If the former, then organizational survival, responsiveness, and accountability should guide nonprofit managers' actions. If the latter, then autonomy, independence, and innovativeness should prevail. Resolution of this issue has obvious implications for the design and philosophy of a nonprofit management curriculum.

Another critical question, at least as old as Plato, is whether, to what extent, and how values can be taught. Should nonprofit management programs bypass values on the assumption that values cannot be taught, at least to adults in formal education settings; or should such programs, through explicit course work or other means, consciously attempt to develop or change the values of participants? A related question is what nonprofit *managerial* values might consist of, as distinguished from the general values desirable for workers and volunteers in the nonprofit sector.

Types of Nonprofit Organizations

Paralleling the discussion of values by conference participants was the suspicion that the nonprofit sector was perhaps not a unified sector at all, but a tripartite sector with significantly different values prevailing in each of the parts. The dominant part, as measured by revenue, expenditures, and employees, is that of *service organizations* that produce health care and social services, education, research, artistic performances and exhibitions, and so on. A second important category is that of *advocacy organizations*, which are normally funded without government or business support and which exist to promote a social cause of some kind. A third category is that of *mutual benefit organizations* such as professional and trade associations and labor unions, whose purposes are to promote economic and related interests of their members.

One education-related question that arises here is whether these divisions have values in common. Are mutual benefit organizations based on the principle of self-interest rather than on some conception of the public interest? Are service organizations essentially driven by the interests of clients and funders? Do advocacy organizations uniquely capture the sector's underlying values of independence, autonomy, and pluralism? And if these divisions are significant, what focus should a university program in nonprofit management take? Or should there be different programs for each category? What are the values of major types of nonprofits, how alike or different are they, and what implications does all this have for nonprofit management curricula?

Mark Keane, Distinguished Visiting Professor in the Department of Public Administration at George Washington University, and Astrid Merget, Director of the School of Public Administration at Ohio State University, discussing the George Washington University Master of Association Management program (which focuses on the mutual benefit category), are unwilling to accept a sharp division between mutual benefit and other classes of nonprofits. Rather, they see mutual benefit organizations advocating their own conceptions of the public interest as well as providing information to the public and services to their members. Other conference participants felt that nonprofit service-producing organizations have not abandoned their advocacy and innovation roles. Finally, O'Connell argues that, despite being a small fraction of the sector, advocacy organizations represent its heart and soul, i.e., the values of pluralism, independence, creativity, and autonomy from the market or from governmental imperatives. Therefore, he says, advocacy organizations should be a prominent focus of nonprofit management curricula, and the values underlying these organizations should be emphasized even for management of service and mutual benefit organizations.

The practical aspects of management also appear to distinguish nonprofits from other kinds of organizations. Bruce Vladeck, President of the United Hospital Fund, points to unique problems in managing boards of trustees, raising capital funds, managing volunteers, and administering compensation systems. While these differences in management bolster the argument for a separate nonprofit curriculum, the nonprofit sector is far from homogeneous. Not only are there value differences among service, advocacy, and mutual benefit organizations, but there are also practical differences in managing nonprofits of vastly different sizes. Jonathan Cook, National Executive Director of the Support Centers of America, grapples with this issue and its educational implications. Cook suggests that a principal concern of small nonprofit organizations is survival and the attainment of a critical level of stable funding. This may require a different curricular emphasis than that appropriate for large nonprofit organizations. Overall, however, Cook argues that offering separate curricula for small and large nonprofit organizations is not practical. First, the required subject matter would not be radically different. Accounting, finance, strategic planning, community politics, and so on, would be relevant for both small and large nonprofits, though the applications would be different. Second, the market would probably not support more than one type of nonprofit education program. Finally, the focus for nonprofit management education should be on careers, not specific organizations or types of organizations. Since nonprofit managers often move from small to large organizations over their careers, it seems unwise to bifurcate the educational system along the lines of organizational size.

Management vs. Leadership

Another fundamental question is whether nonprofit management education programs ought to be developing managers or leaders. Leaders are thought to set new directions, define the issues, and galvanize their followers to act on behalf of new initiatives. Managers, as a rough stereotype, keep things running smoothly, efficiently, and effectively. These alternative conceptions reflect the value issues discussed above and also have important educational implications. Should a nonprofit management curriculum emphasize managerial controls and the maximizing of organizational performance, or should it stress problem-solving and creative thinking skills and emphasize liberal studies and issue awareness?

If the purpose of a nonprofit management program is to train leaders, then the latter educational orientation may be more appropriate. Vladeck points to the classical training given leaders in ancient Chinese dynasties and the British Empire. Other conference participants argued that while the techniques of management could be taught, it was questionable whether leadership could actually be taught. On this issue, however, Richard Cyert, President of Carnegie-Mellon University, argues that it is possible to teach leadership strategies that can be used effectively in complex nonprofit institutions such as universities, hospitals, and other organizations in which the command and control structure is loosely defined. Cyert develops the notion of "attention focus," which consists of various ways in which the leader of an organization can get the membership to concentrate its attention on specific problems. In so doing, the membership can be energized by being given a key role in policy formulation and a stake in policy outcomes, while the leader can move the organization in certain desired directions.

Curriculum, Instruction, and Programmatic Issues

Base Within the University. If nonprofit management programs are to be established as something apart from professional clinical education, under what auspices should they be established within the university? Levy argues against containing nonprofit management programs within business schools or schools of public administration, as he argued against containing nonprofit management within clinical professional schools. Although business and public administration schools do see management as their business, Levy, citing his own experiences with university politics, asserts that nonprofit management would be neglected within these larger, dominating, and differently focused units. Furthermore, nonprofit management study has its own legitimacy both in terms of a body of theoretical, managerial, and empirical knowledge and in terms of special constituencies in the philanthropic and service sectors of the economy. Cyert, a former business school professor and dean, argues against locating nonprofit management programs within business schools, on the grounds that business faculty and curricula are so heavily oriented toward the for-profit world that the interests of nonprofit students would be neglected, and that many students would be lost to the nonprofit program as they make salary comparisons between business and nonprofit graduates. Cyert says that public policy or public administration schools are the most appropriate locations for nonprofit management education because of their closeness to the idea of public service. Keane and Merget argue that the stringent accreditation requirements for business schools and schools of public administration would require nonprofit management students to take a substantial amount of course work irrelevant to their interests if nonprofit management were simply a concentration in such fields.

Others at the conference expressed reservations about establishing nonprofit management as something completely new or independent. One set of considerations concerned university politics and economics. Could nonprofit management attract enough students to justify a whole curriculum of its own? Would "rival" management programs such as business or public administration allow this third approach to compete? What are the implications of creating new degrees (e.g., a Master of Nonprofit Administration) versus utilizing recognized degrees such as the MBA or MPA? Are not the latter degrees more credible and hence more valuable to nonprofit management students, despite the possible limitations of their curricula? Moreover, as Keane and Merget argue, is it not better for a young person to obtain a general management degree with established credibility (an MBA or MPA) in order to enhance career opportunities and flexibility? A related question is whether a degree in nonprofit management should be reserved for mid-career professionals already committed to nonprofit careers and sure of their need for specific training in the nuances of nonprofit organizations.

Curriculum. In a sense the entire conference was about the curriculum issue, including whether there could or should be a separate nonprofit management education curriculum and, if so, what it should be. Our thesis throughout has been that the characteristics of nonprofit organizations and the characteristics of nonprofit organization management must be the dominant force shaping any curriculum to meet the needs of these managers.

DiMaggio and others insist on this empirical approach to constructing the nonprofit curriculum. And such an approach, after all, follows the classic principle of occupational training and professional education, that curricula must to some degree flow from the characteristics of the role or occupation. In this context, Arlene Daniels, Professor of Sociology at Northwestern University, traces the emerging role of the private foundation executive; while the extremely small number of such nonprofit workers and the uniqueness of foundation jobs may limit the applicability of these findings to the generic nonprofit management question, such role analysis is central to the curriculum development issue.

While there was general agreement that the nonprofit management curriculum should attend to the issue of values in the nonprofit world and should include general courses in management theory and organizational behavior, the conference produced little consensus as to what specific elements should be included in nonprofit programs. Participants found this lack of consensus neither surprising nor disturbing, given the newness of the field and the necessity for experimentation and further development.

Students. There was some attention in the papers and discussions to the question of appropriate student characteristics for nonprofit management programs. Robert F. Leduc, President of the Institute for Nonprofit Organization Management in Denver, and Terry W. McAdam, until his tragic death in September 1986 the Executive Vice President of the Conrad N. Hilton Foundation, argue that the principal emphasis should be on master's level programs, with some attention to the undergraduate and doctoral levels. Several conference participants noted that most of the current activity is on the master's level and directed toward mid-career nonprofit professionals. Most agreed that the master's degree should be the centerpiece of university-based nonprofit management programs. But there was some discussion of alternatives at the doctoral level as well. One argument for the doctorate was that many nonprofit managers come from the ranks of professions in which they have already received master's degrees (e.g., MSWs) and would be reluctant to take another one. Alternately, it seemed impractical to combine a rigorous management concentration with already demanding professional master's degree curricula. A doctoral degree would thus be an attractive alternative. However, conference participants such as Slavin argued that such a degree should not be research-oriented like the Ph.D. but should be a practitioner's doctorate. One participant half-facetiously suggested the DNA (doctor of nonprofit administration) as a "lively" alternative.

Although current programs and this conference and book are directed toward managers of nonprofit organizations, some conference participants suggested attention to other key decision-makers in the nonprofit sector. One such group is nonprofit board members. We noted earlier the exceptional importance of boards in nonprofit organizations. If these individuals do not have a good understanding of their roles in the organization or if they do not appreciate the nuances of nonprofit work, they can frustrate even the best-trained managers. It was suggested, therefore, that universities might turn their attention to educating board members.

Similarly, it was observed by Arthur Blum, Acting Director of the Mandel Center for Non-Profit Organizations at Case Western Reserve University, that nonprofit service organizations commonly operate in a web of funding and regulatory systems and networks of peer organizations, and that many nonprofit organizations themselves are structured as systems—federations, associations, and so on—rather than unified corporate bodies. Thus, Blum suggested that universities ought to consider educating nonprofit *system* managers as well as single-organization managers.

Faculty. Who should teach in nonprofit management programs? Leduc and McAdam argue for a mix of full-time and adjunct faculty as well as a mix of full-time faculty from several different departments within the university. Most conference participants agreed that some mix of full-time and part-time faculty was desirable, but precisely what the mix should be requires further investigation and probably tailoring to the requirements of particular university programs.

SUMMARY OF CONFERENCE CONCLUSIONS

While the conference and book were intended to be exploratory rather than to produce consensus, certain general areas of agreement nonetheless emerged from the papers and discussion. Some of the major conclusions are the following:

- There is now a strong interest in, considerable latent demand for, and some experience with university-based programs of nonprofit management education.
- There is something distinctive about nonprofit organizations in comparison with business and government organizations, in terms of the way they operate, their legal foundations, and the philosophies on which they are based.
- There is an emerging body of social science and managerial knowledge that forms an intellectual basis of sufficient stature to command respect and warrant separate development in the university setting.
- There is no "one best way" to do nonprofit management education, based on the experience and analysis of the present time. Several important models have already emerged—the concentration within the MBA degree, the concentration within the MPA degree, the Master of Nonprofit Administration (MNA) degree, discipline-based programs in the arts, education, social work, religion, etc.—and these and other models need to be tested over time. It is too early to narrow the field down to one model.
- Nonprofit management programs should be responsive to local needs as well as to the parameters of the nonprofit management role and management theory in general.

• Nonprofit management programs should follow the experience of the best professional education programs in combining theory and research with practice, and in including both full-time research-oriented faculty and part-time practitioner faculty in the program delivery.

2

Curing Benign Neglect: Alternative Approaches to Nonprofit Management Education

Reynold Levy

The formulation and execution of graduate education programs for managers of nonprofit organizations is riddled with practical and pedagogical questions. On the practical side, the market to be served is complex and highly differentiated. Will a given curriculum be framed to serve part-time or full-time students? Current or aspiring program managers (in social work, health care, education, advocacy and community organization, the arts), functional managers (in finance, marketing, development, public relations, human resources), or chief executive officers?

Should consideration be given to the cultivation of a student body composed in part of volunteers and board members? Will the offerings lead to an advanced degree in generic nonprofit management, a certificate for the completion of a course of study, an effective "concentration" within a traditional advanced program, and/or continuing education for full-time workers as a supplement to in-service training and to courses sponsored by service organizations and professional associations?

Is it anticipated that the cost of student education will be subsidized by the nonprofit place of work or constitute principally a student investment in knowledge and career opportunity? Does the program regard its reach to students as national, regional, or local? Will it be lodged as a major, serious concentration alternative in an acknowledged discipline (law, business, public administration, social work) or treated as a new, free-standing course of study? Is teaching the major objective of the program, or will research, conferences, and technical assistance to nonprofit institutions be regarded as useful (critical) features of the undertaking?

These pragmatic questions are surely among those confronting any college or university assessing its role in the education and training of nonprofit managers. In combination, they call for a careful exercise in market differentiation and the construction of an academic program that flows from the situational and intellectual strengths of a given institution. That is a managerial exercise best left to those professors and administrators whose hands are on the pulse of their campus and their community. Here it is best to pose, not seize, the challenge. Instead, in what follows, attention will be drawn to a pedagogical debate: Is there a body of knowledge and set of skills intrinsic to nonprofit management that is sufficiently distinctive to justify a dedicated core curriculum or concentration? If so, what might it look like?

DISCIPLINE IS DESTINY

The issues raised by these pedagogical questions are not easily resolved. Fundamentally, two perspectives dominate a continuing exchange of views and are worth some articulation.

There are those who contend that no curriculum offering distant from the disciplines in which successful managers must be well grounded and nurtured can possibly command the respect of the nonprofit marketplace. From this point of view, the particular substance of a nonprofit agency (what it does, the specific business it is in) is always more important than its sectoral status (nonprofit vs. for-profit or government). It follows that graduate education must be rooted in traditional professional experience and credentialing, not in a generic nonprofit course of study. The notion that one can be trained to perform program or functional management capably across disciplines is regarded by most practitioners in any given field as highly unrealistic.

Apart from distinctions arising from professional identity and role (program vs. functional manager), a nonprofit institution can be plotted by other key characteristics, such as size, budget, and the degree to which its operation resembles that of a government agency, a "free-market" enterprise, some mixture of the two, or something best characterized on its own terms.

In this view the sectoral auspice of an agency has little explanatory power. Indeed, in many if not all fields, every sector is represented by institutions competing for a given market. Consider the commingling of for-profit, nonprofit, and public hospitals, nursing homes, day care centers, health maintenance organizations, universities, and primary and secondary schools—to cite a few illustrations. That mix in the marketplace and the likely movement of professionals within a given discipline renders any effort to train by sectoral perspective futile.

This camp maintains, therefore, that while there may be room to infuse in the core curriculum of traditional disciplines whatever managerial and behavioral distinctions arise from the dynamics of a nonprofit status, any such differences are of degree, not kind. As such, they are unworthy of discrete, generic treatment.

A graduating student educated in health administration can possibly work with equal ease in the human resources department of a Fortune 500 company, in a public hospital, or in a nonprofit ambulatory setting. A functional manager trained in "generic" nonprofit marketing, on the other hand, probably cannot "sell" tickets, beds, tuition, fees, and government contracts across varying fields with a similar measure of comfort, competence, and confidence.

In sum, discipline is destiny. The skilled program professional needs a graduate *education* to operate successfully in any setting. The nonprofit management skills needed can be conveyed within the four corners of that discipline or learned while on the job. That's called *training*. The law school educates, the law firm trains. A business school educates; the company, investment firm, consultant outfit, trains.

Practically and pedagogically there is no other way. To proceed down another path would do no less than deny or trivialize the substance of time-tested academic programs in social work, education, religion, and health care, among other fields. It would confuse academic rigor with vocationalism. The latter is either built on the foundation of the former or it has no place in an institution devoted not to technique or career incubation and development, but to the discovery and transmission of knowledge.

THE SECTORAL IMPERATIVE

There is another view worth scrutiny. For, whatever the current marketplace may appear to dictate in educational preference for hiring purposes, the environment of most nonprofits has fundamentally changed. Government budget reduction. Growing service demands. Undiminished competition and regulation. The prospect, for many, of flat if not declining contributions. It is and will remain a time of turbulence when agencies can ill afford the luxury of prolonged and inadequate on-the-job training while its program managers evolve into able functional managers.

The new expectations of boards of directors for performance-based measures of efficiency and effectiveness, and concomitant demands for entrepreneurial, planning, fundraising, marketing, budgetary, and personnel skills of a high order, may meet a disappointing response in the ranks of program administrators. Ruling out pools of talent educated in unorthodox ways is an option that few institutions can afford to exercise.

Indeed, just as many hospitals no longer find a trained physician in the top administrative role and just as universities no longer turn exclusively to pedigreed provosts or deans in presidential searches, so too those educated in first–class, generic nonprofit management may well find surprising acceptance in the marketplace.

Consider the arts. The last two administrative directors of the Metropolitan Museum of New York have been former career diplomats. The Los Angeles Music Center also turned to the foreign service for its chief executive officer. The Kennedy Center for the Performing Arts is run by a businessman. The Lincoln Center for the Performing Arts is led by a lawyer and former first deputy mayor of the city of New York. The Field Museum in Chicago and the Metropolitan Opera of New York turned for their chiefs of staff respectively to the former president of the University of Iowa and a former senior executive in a major advertising agency.

These illustrations, easily multiplied, suggest that even without generic training a number of boards of directors at leading institutions presume that management experience is transferable not only across disciplines within the nonprofit sector but across sectors. Truth to tell, one of the many understudied subjects of nonprofit behavior is the professional and educational background, the tenure and the patterns of mobility of managers in such institutions, large and small.

Whatever those data would reveal, it is not unreasonable to assume that unconventional paths to high–level posts might widen if high-quality generic education in nonprofit management were to become a respected course of study in American higher education. In fact, executive search firms report that demand is greater than supply for nonprofit manangers who can fill development, marketing, and finance posts. Generic nonprofit management education can help fill that gap.

Assuming, *arguendo*, a reasonable marketplace acceptance of its graduates, is there a defensible, pedagogical case for a course of study in generic nonprofit management? Its advocates contend that the current state of management training in the nonprofit field via so-called concentrations is woefully deficient. Traditional disciplines rarely utilize or develop case material derived from nonprofit realities, rarely utilize full-time or adjunct faculty who have current or recent experience as practitioners—rarely, in short, approach third sector institutions on their own merits. Rather, the preponderance of work is on the discipline or sector demarcated for attention. Nonprofit dynamics tend to be treated as derivatives of or variations on a given management theme, skill, or technique. Social work, business, public administration, law are the dogs—the nonprofit sector, a short tail.

While these deficiencies can be remedied within the confines of a traditional curriculum, it is to be doubted that a faculty committed to a given educational mission and methodology can easily welcome a genuine integration of a different body of knowledge and skills.

JUSTIFYING THE GENERIC

What are the features of nonprofit institutions across program disciplines that distinguish themselves sufficiently to justify a separate, dedicated approach to their study? One might begin with the historical, philosophical, and religious roots of nonprofit institutions and their consequent tradition-blessed, unique role in American civic and intellectual life. How they originated, what functions they perform in the body politic, and how they contribute to the exercise of freedom, the preservation of pluralism, and the prevention of both state tyranny and unbridled free enterprise are well worth examination. From the *Federalist Papers* to Alexis de Toqueville, from John Winthrop to Peter Berger, from Moses Maimonides to Robert Nisbet, Waldemar Nielsen, or John Gardner, there is in the stuff of the third sector a rich vein of practice and theory to be tapped.

Critical to pedagogical justification is an appreciation for the traits that conceptually and practically mark off the third sector from the first sector (free enterprise) and the second (government). What is the legal framework of nonprofits' institutional creation and operations? What is the special manner in which they are governed and the unique set of interactions that condition board-staff relationships? How are their missions to be distinguished from the demands of the bottom line and the ballot box? What services do nonprofits provide to render them an important force in America's economy?

Their scope and impact, as measured by operating and capital budgets, asset values, employment, philanthropic giving in cash and volunteers, all command attention. What accounts for the vitality of this slice of the American economy, estimated to employ 10 percent of those working and one of every six white-collar jobs, to own 11 percent of the value of all the country's real estate, to spend on the order of $250 billion annually, and to attract $80 billion in contributed funds and a multiple of that figure in the dollar value of the volunteer time of millions?

How do the labor-intensive, tax-exempt, volunteer-dependent, and public-purpose qualities of nonprofits condition management processes and outcomes? Of what special significance is their capacity to receive tax-deductible gifts and to be utilized heavily by government as a service provider?

How do the competing needs for efficiency and equity, participation and direction, policy determination and operational implementation, exercising authority and building consensus and accommodation play themselves out as between the board of directors, staff, and volunteers in a structure of governance foreign to most who labor in for-profit and government arenas?

What are the distinctive factors that shape how nonprofits measure effectiveness (unit costs of service vs. operating margins and net profit, the ratio of endowment resources to the size of the operating budget vs. the exercise of taxing power, levels of membership involvement vs. voter participation rates), or how they approach marketing and sales challenges (use of subsidized direct mail/direct response vs. franking of newsletters and correspondence), or how they develop budgets, control costs, improve productivity, or handle management-union relationships?

These dimensions of nonprofit organizational dynamics may, in fact, be differences of kind and not degree. Or, to put the matter another way, they at least constitute differences of such degree from their government and for-profit counterparts and are of such historical and contemporary importance that dedicated study seems fully warranted. Surely, fundraising, generating earned income, negotiating third-party purchase of service contracts, and complying with regulatory edicts in the nonprofit sector demand a set of skills and a temperament somewhat foreign to managers at Boeing, the Pentagon, or the local social service administration office. Surely, working with a nonprofit board and volunteers is distinguishable from reporting to a board of directors over which one presides and exerts control, or to the general electorate. And, surely, financial management and resource development in nonprofit organizations suggest the need for special education and training.

The history, philosophy, sociology, economics, politics, and management of nonprofits demand far more than treating them as a tributary or derivative of, or deviation from, government and business. Colleges and universities today too often treat nonprofits in this way—interstitially, filling spaces in a curriculum dedicated to other purposes, driven by other needs. There is another, perhaps a better way.

That such cognitive territory and management skills justify head-on treatment seems clear. But can a generic nonprofit management curriculum command a respectable and respected place in the firmament of graduate degree programs at leading universities?

YES, IF

There must be a university commitment at the highest level to the utilization of the best department-based faculty to participate in an interdisciplinary advanced management program on nonprofit institutions. Concurrently, the attraction of a high-quality chairperson, as well as, full-time tenured, untenured, and adjunct faculty is necessary. Nonprofit executives in residence, team teaching, internships and apprenticeships in voluntary organizations should also be seriously entertained.

Taking such steps requires setting aside and raising ample resources to stay the course. It requires rigor in the selection of those who teach, high academic standards for curriculum content, and substantial funds for course development. Also needed is a careful blending of professional backgrounds for those appointed to counsel students, to conduct research, to establish and maintain relationships with nonprofit institutions, and to interpret the educational mission of this new management program to its various publics. In these efforts, striking the right balance of the theoretical and the practical is of great importance.

The threshold questions limned earlier about the target student body, the range of activities to be conducted, and the scope of the curriculum demand careful deliberation. It is doubtful that an advanced degree program in nonprofit management can succeed without field–specific seminars, clinical sequences to grapple with real institutional problems and examine fresh case material, and well–supervised field work experiences. The open–textured quality of the third sector and the novelty of higher education attending to its management needs are already leading to a variety of experiments in how best to attract students, faculty, and research staff. That is as it should be.

But a critical ingredient for the success of almost any such endeavor must be the capacity to connect meaningfully with nonprofit institutions and to satisfy concerns articulated by their leadership. For it is they that are the sources of employment for graduating students, the living laboratories for student learning and, given their training needs and expertise, an important market to tap both for tuition subsidy and part-time faculty. The success of many business schools in offering MBAs and executive education programs is attributable in no small measure to their strong linkages with the local, regional, or national corporate community. Nothing less is needed for a set of authentic, mutually advantageous interactions with third sector organizations.

Will the university-based nonprofit management program be blessed with a staff and faculty possessed of the background and drive, and provided with the resources and incentives to cultivate such relationships? No small challenge. No mean task.

Professorial resistance will be high. Those who believe that discipline is destiny possess powerful intellectual arguments, no less so because they are often contained in luggage accurately labeled "the protection and advancement of self-interest." The strong disciplinary orientation of the university is embodied in a potent departmental structure, jealous of its prerogatives, certain of its ground, wary of newcomers, and eager for any incremental resources. These forces militate strongly against enduring cooperative initiatives across disciplinary lines. They develop the strongest of antibodies when confronted with proposals for a novel, free-standing program.

Battle-weary proponents of black, women's, and environmental studies would identify strongly with Hans Morgenthau's observation that Lord Acton was wrong. It is not power that corrupts. It is the absence of power. The proof? The tough "politics" of departmental wrangling at most American colleges and universities.

The sectoral imperative runs head on into the rock of a reward and status system still strongly oriented to research rather than teaching, to the advancement of academic fields that transcend the university itself, rendering inconsequential the realization of a role in local community improvement, to tenure and the tenure-tracked rather than adjuncts, and to the next manuscript or maybe the classroom, but not the world(s) of work.

If those obstacles seem formidable, advocates of a more spacious, imaginative, dedicated, and direct approach to nonprofit management should take comfort in the axiom: it was ever thus. For behind the development of many now established, consensus-blessed disciplines, indeed whole schools (of thought as well as of students, faculty, and degrees), was struggle—for legitimacy, visibility, a place in the pecking order of preexisting institutional priorities.

A DONOR'S PERSPECTIVE

Eighty billion dollars—that's what individual Americans, foundations, and corporations donated to nonprofit institutions in 1985. What did those contributions buy? Through whose hands does that money flow? How capable and dexterous are they? To whom are nonprofit managers accountable for expenditures of significant magnitude, and how prepared are the fiduciaries of those funds—boards of directors—to discharge their responsibilities with knowledge and integrity?

In San Francisco, 3,450 nonprofit institutions employing 35,000 people spent $2.5 billion in 1982 (Harder, Kimmich, and Salamon 1985). That level of expenditure equalled roughly twice the budget of the city of San Francisco. In New York City, Salamon finds, the figures are comparably impressive: 6,659 nonprofit organizations employing 351,000 people spent $16.5 billion (Grossman, Salamon and Altschuler 1986). That level of expenditure in 1982 was $1 billion more than the budget of the city of New York and that level of employment was one and a half times the size of the entire municipal workforce.

Will anyone be heard to quarrel with the view that the citizens of San Francisco and New York City deserve some managers trained in the art and science of public (i.e., government) administration? Yet one can search in vain for a single university prepared to defend the view that its nonprofit management offerings currently nurture graduates capable of wielding resources and delivering services of at least comparable size and consequence on behalf of the third sector. The disparity is stark.

Attracting, retaining, educating, and training the very best talent for the nation's nonprofit service sector is critical to securing the full benefit of philanthropic investments. Lay leaders and professional staff laboring in nonprofit vineyards merit educational programs designed and delivered with imagination, vigor, and intelligence.

The prospect of elements of American higher education embracing that charge is exciting. Whether educational innovation takes the form of major alterations in existing curricula, the creation of new, free-standing advanced degree programs, or course work supplemental to in-service and continuing education matters less than undertaking to help fill this major void.

One of the hallmarks of American culture is its pluralism. Multiple sources of energetic problem-solving and opportunity-seizing is the American way. Undoubtedly, that diversity will reflect itself in the heterogeneous approaches to nonprofit management education now being nurtured across the country. In that context, the guiding principles and questions posed here may be of some use. Unless those who run and govern nonprofits are infused with an understanding of philanthropic tradition, possessed of an appreciation of the distinctive role of the third sector, and equipped with the management skills to properly discharge their responsibilities, it is unlikely that donations, government support, and growing levels of earned income will proceed apace.

Precisely how or under what auspice these objectives are met matters less than that they are recognized and addressed with a level of investment that begins to approach that with which other disciplines are favored. Those who value our country's "mediating structures" cannot but sense that the stakes are high and the challenge significant.

3

The Place of Nonprofit Management Programs in Higher Education

Richard M. Cyert

For many years prior to the end of World War II, the approach to management education tended to be quite specific with respect to institutions and industries. There was a heavy emphasis in the business school programs on education for particular industries. Thus, it was not surprising to find in various schools programs for management of chemical industries, for management of construction firms, and so on. The idea seemed to be that the techniques and approaches that might be taught were peculiar to a particular industry. The tendency was to avoid generalization. In fields such as accounting, the idea was further reinforced. Business schools had courses that taught accounting for particular industries.

That philosophy began to change after World War II. An increased number of business schools began teaching general management. The idea that there were general principles and techniques in management that were valid regardless of the industry or the institution began to prevail. Even specialized institutional programs such as hospital management and public administration began to adopt the same kinds of courses and techniques that were being taught in the business schools. It was recognized that there was a great deal of overlap in the knowledge that was necessary for a manager in any industry or any institution to have.

An information processing theory of management began to be developed. This theory recognized that management was an art and not a science. As an art, management implied the use of judgment. In order to develop informed judgment, it was necessary for the manager to have access to a number of different bodies of knowledge. Therefore, the education for a manager consisted of teaching those disciplines and giving the student experience in retrieving information from the various bodies of knowledge. The knowledge was then applied to the solution of problems as part of the educational process. This approach made it possible to teach management as an academic topic, and it enabled the principles of management to be spread to other fields.

NATURE OF MANAGEMENT OF NONPROFIT ORGANIZATIONS

Despite the importance of nonprofit organizations, little attention has been given to them by management scholars. The tendency has been to emphasize the business firm without looking for the possible transfer of knowledge to other institutions. Nonprofit organizations producing important services, including foundations, child care centers, hospitals, universities, and cultural organizations, have largely been ignored. There has been no attempt to transfer the knowledge of the general management literature to these organizations. The importance of these nonprofits makes the study of managing them critical.

Anyone who has discussed management with practicing managers recognizes that each manager believes that his or her business and problems are unique. Managers of any organization, profit or nonprofit, believe that the training required for the management must be unique. If this view were accepted, we would obviously have a large number of specialized management schools. It is this philosophy that has changed since World War II.

An organization of any kind is developed to achieve certain goals or objectives by group activity. These objectives are ones that individuals working alone cannot achieve or objectives for which it can be argued that there are economies of scale. Therefore, it is more economical to achieve these tasks by working within an organization. More specifically, every organization is designed to produce a solution to a problem of society. The word "problem" is used in a broad sense but calls attention to the fact that organizations—whether they produce candy bars or educational services or collect dimes to stamp out disease—are attempting to provide solutions to a problem. It is interesting to apply this same concept to illegal organizations. In many cases the point is still valid—numbers rackets, prostitution rings—the solution, however, is not desired by society and is made illegal. In other cases the illegal organization is designed to produce a solution to a problem, and the problem is not one that is recognized by society (for example, organizations for providing assassinations). These objectives of an organization are an accurate description of whether the organization is a nonprofit or profit-making organization. The achievement of the organization's objectives can generally be described as being dependent upon the production of services or material goods. Goods or services are produced to fulfill the organization's objectives. Given the scarcity of resources, all organizations, whether profit or nonprofit, should want to produce the goods or services in the most efficient way. Thus, it is necessary to find the techniques for producing and distributing the goods and services that will use the least amount of society's resources—measured by the monetary value that society places on the resources.

There is some discussion in the literature that might cast doubt on this proposition. It is argued that nonprofits may lack the incentives to minimize cost or they may desire to address the "expressive" needs of their members (Mason 1984). Neither of these points, however, contradicts the proposition. There is evidence with profit-making firms that they are not always minimum-cost producers because other objectives may interfere with the minimum cost objective. When a firm is prosperous, organizational slack accumulates as various subgroups in the organization attempt to capture more of the resources for themselves to ease the workload. Unless an organization, profit or nonprofit, always has more resources than it needs to achieve its objectives, there will always be pressure to reduce cost. In particular, as the pressure to cut costs is applied in the organization, less attention is given to addressing expressive needs of members and more to satisfying the basic objectives of the organization.

Obviously, one can extend this type of reasoning to show the close similarity between profit and nonprofit organizations. There are certainly differences, but the real question is whether these differences require any differences in the training that needs to be given to prospective managers for the two sectors.

Perhaps the major difference that most business people would allude to in distinguishing their organizations from nonprofit organizations would be the evaluation process. The business person would point to the bottom line and indicate that performance can be judged by the bottom line, whereas there is no such bottom line for evaluative purposes in the nonprofit organization. Initially this point seems to indicate a great difference between the two kinds of organizations, but in reality it does not. It is possible to develop performance measures for the nonprofit organization as well. Specifically, we need to measure the quality of the services provided by the nonprofit organization in relation to the cost of those services. There needs to be some kind of agreement on the methods for measurement by both the top management of the organization and those managers responsible for the delivery of these services. Thus, in a university it is necessary for the president and the deans to arrive at a mutually satisfactory measurement system that will evaluate the performance of each dean. In a hospital, the hospital management and the physician practitioners must arrive at an operational definition of quality medical care.

The difficulty lies in defining the quality of the performance for nonprofits. In a profit-making organization, the market evaluates the performance. In a nonprofit, it is necessary to determine the quality of the product given the constraint of available funds. This measurement usually involves tension between the professionals involved and those managing the resources.

The point is that it is possible to develop measures of performance for nonprofits that can be used just as the measure of profit and loss is used in the for-profit organization (Harvey and Snyder 1987).

DESIRABLE MANAGERIAL TRAINING

The education should be for professional management. It should be based on the underlying disciplines that the student will use as a manager. The training should not be modified significantly from the education of a business manager even though the student may spend most of his or her professional life in a nonprofit organization. Thus, there should be no diminution of the time spent on developing analytical skills or knowledge of the behavioral sciences, or even of the knowledge of some of the fundamental areas of business, such as finance and marketing. Accounting should be emphasized. On this score it is interesting to note that the whole trend of financial statements in universities, where fund accounting prevails, is toward making the statements of the universities more closely resemble those of business organizations (Bastable 1973).

The manager of the nonprofit organization must be trained in the same underlying disciplines and resource-allocating skills as a prospective business manager. In particular it is important to stress the area of developing strategy for an organization (Keller 1983). This area is one that has been stressed in business schools. It is equally critical for nonprofit organizations since their long-run survival also depends upon economic factors. Thus, nonprofit organizations must do some long-range planning to help insure their viability. The declaration of desirable goals is not enough to guarantee immortality.

Courses dealing with the "institutional" aspects of specific kinds of nonprofit organization must be included in the curriculum. The need for elaborating on the special characteristics of a foundation or an arts organization is particularly important. The student must have an understanding of the special features of the particular nonprofit to be able to apply the general techniques of management more effectively. It would obviously be foolish to apply a linear programming transportation model to the itinerary of a symphony orchestra on tour in the same way that one might schedule trucks transporting ketchup from factories to warehouses.

At the same time, the curriculum should not overemphasize this aspect of nonprofits. There are characteristics that must be emphasized in the classroom and others that will be quickly learned on the job. Also, we must be careful to avoid falling into the trap of early business education where it was believed that the student had to be educated for particular industries.

CHARACTERISTICS OF NONPROFIT ORGANIZATIONS

The problem of developing good evaluations of performance has been mentioned. Without some kind of measurement, however, there is a real danger of never knowing when a nonprofit organization is functioning well. Part of the problem of evaluation stems from the differing expectations of the various constituencies. Thus, as Cohen and March (1974) point out for universities, there is no agreement among trustees, faculty, and students on the criteria for judging the performance of the president.

Another aspect of the evaluation problem is the fact that many nonprofits are shielded from the effects of the market. This condition is true for governmental organizations. Here the major reliance is on criticisms by the opposition party. Frequently, however, these criticisms are so biased as to be discounted and in any event are given in a context where the management has to become defensive. It is, therefore, necessary for any nonprofit organization to develop the kind of feedback mechanisms that will give it an adequate measurement of its performance. To some extent, when the nonprofit organization is in a competitive market—for example, private universities—the market will function through the number of students that enroll and through the ability of the organization to hire and to hold outstanding faculty members. Even in this case the market is not a completely valid evaluation mechanism because it reacts slowly to declines in quality. A university can develop a strong reputation that has a half-life of long duration. No serious efforts have been made to measure such time periods, but a twenty-year half-life is not unreasonable (Margulies and Blau 1973; most knowledgeable business school observers, I believe, would challenge the rankings presented). Thus, it is useful to develop feedback mechanisms on performance in other ways. Sometimes this feedback can come through comparisons of financial data with other institutions. Sometimes the feedback mechanism can operate by establishing a group of organizations that can compare operations. This approach is usually inadequate because innovative developments are kept hidden, and therefore the competing organizations will not be made aware of such developments. The best device is probably an internal mechanism which takes the responsibility. It may be, for example, a committee to develop criteria for evaluating performance. Such a committee can frequently be aided by an outside consultant, but the necessity to look at procedures for evaluation of performance by an objective committee can be an effective way of providing the kind of feedback that is necessary. However, such an approach is probably more effective for particular subunits than it is for the organization as a whole.

More important, changes in traditional methods—for example, the introduction of new technological processes—most easily develop throughout the leadership of the top management of the organization. It is difficult in universities to achieve productivity increases of significance. The nature of the organization tends to insulate it from change unless there is some institutionalized device for stimulating it. The written and unwritten rules of academic freedom which prevent class visitation and analysis of the classroom educational process by an outside group, inhibit change even though such rules may be necessary for other purposes. There is ample evidence, for example, that universities are in need of methods to improve their productivity in delivering educational services (Dubin and Taveggia 1968, pp. 1–10). Unfortunately, there is no clear way of achieving these improvements. Some things can be done in a particular college, but generally, a new mechanism that will affect incentives is necessary to achieve change at the university level. Sometimes change will be forced on the organization when survival depends upon improved productivity. We need to find devices that will function as stimulants for the introduction of new ideas and for the quicker adoption of new technologies. We need organizational mechanisms that will provide the same stimulus as the market provides firms in competitive markets.

One of the keys to increasing productivity is to persuade all the participants in the organization—especially faculty and students—to incorporate the goal in their own goal structure. One potential source of change in the administration process flows from the professionalization of management in nonprofit organizations and the pressures for change in the professional organizations to which these managers belong. Thus, accounting organizations stimulated the introduction of computers into business firms. It became clear that the accounting tasks could be done more effectively with computers, and the potential improved quality became a basis for professionals in the accounting area to demand the increased investment from their top managements. This kind of activity is consistent with the functions of professional societies. One of their major roles is to keep the practicing professional current with the most advanced practices. There is, of course, always the danger that the practices, while advanced, may not produce benefits greater than the costs (*Unlocking the computer's profit potential*, 1968, pp. 1–38).

In addition, we must remember that the objectives of the nonprofit organization are the production of services—educational, governmental, health, cultural, and so on. In the desire to achieve an efficient allocation of resources, the manager of the nonprofit organization must be careful not to destroy the essential nature of the organization. There is a balance that must be maintained between the efficiency of resource allocation and the effective achievement of the delivery and production of the services. In general, nonprofit organizations are populated by professionals, and the emphasis on economic efficiency frequently results in some assault on the ideals and mores of these professionals. This factor must be borne in mind while at the same time attempting to manage the organization efficiently.

DESIGN OF ORGANIZATION

Nonprofit organizations generally tend to be centralized. This tendency is not accidental. The basis for a decentralized design in business firms is the profit-center concept. As we have seen, such a concept is generally difficult to implement in nonprofit organizations (Chandler 1966, pp. 158–199). If a nonprofit organization is decentralized, it is usually because of a weak central administration that merely turns budget funds over to decentralized units without attempting to evaluate performance. In universities, in particular, it is fashionable to talk about running with each tub on its own bottom. This approach, however, is generally followed only when the individual colleges are separately endowed. When such endowment is not available, it is more difficult to operate on a decentralized basis because of the lack of ability to make performance measurements other than the fiscal one, whether or not the unit lives within its budget. Therefore, a good manager will tend to centralize the organization and determine the goals the organization should achieve.

As we have argued, there is a need to design performance measures for individual units. When such concepts can be developed it may be possible to operate nonprofit organizations in a decentralized fashion in the same way that profit-making organizations can be operated in a decentralized manner based on the profit-center concept. Without some indices of performance it is difficult to know when a unit has performed badly other than fiscally.

In addition to the difficulty of measurement, a decentralized design runs into the difficulty of finding a large enough number of good managers to operate the organization effectively. It is obvious that a decentralized organization will need more people who can manage independently. American business firms have been able to decentralize because of the supply of managerial talent. The supply is adequate in part because of the large number of business schools in the country. Even though these schools may not have been great academically, they have served to attract people to the management area as a profession. This fact has resulted in a better supply of managers than in countries like the United Kingdom or the U.S.S.R., where no management education of significance existed until relatively recently. The difficulties of attempting to run an organization in a decentralized manner with inadequate managerial talent should be clear. The conflicts that arise between the staff and line managers in such an organization make it difficult for it to function. In a properly designed decentralized organization the staff organization should be composed of specialists, who are too expensive to have in large numbers. The organization needs only a few, centrally located and used intensively. Thus, because of the inadequate supply of managers and lack of performance evaluation criteria, most well-managed nonprofit organizations tend toward a centralized design.

MANAGEMENT INNOVATION IN NONPROFIT ORGANIZATIONS

It is necessary to look at the sources of revenue for nonprofits in order to understand why they have not been as innovative in the past as profit-making organizations. The revenue for nonprofits has come from taxes in the form of subsidies to the organization, from endowment income where the endowment has been in the organization for some time, from gifts, from insurance payments, and other such sources. In other words, the revenue system has generally been one in which the nonprofit is not required to reduce its costs, improve its product, or develop a better delivery system to benefit from the revenue. In fact, the amount of revenue raised was frequently related to the level of deficit incurred. The nonprofit that runs a deficit may have an easier time raising money than one showing a surplus. For the business firm, lack of profit has the effect of putting pressure on the organization to increase its revenues. Thus, if the firm operates at a loss, new methods for increasing revenue as well as for decreasing costs must be developed. In the case of nonprofits there has not been the same need to increase revenue and decrease costs. As a result, nonprofit organizations have lacked the pressure that leads to problem-oriented research and to innovation (Cyert and March 1963, pp. 278–279). It is therefore not surprising that we have seen a much greater drive toward innovative techniques in profit-making organizations than in nonprofit ones.

In addition, in nonprofit organizations—and this is particularly true of government—the term of office frequently is too short for the organization to take the long-term approach to problems necessary for innovating. Pressure is much heavier on short-term performance when there is no long-term commitment to the organization. The faculty member on tenure and the government worker on civil service have a long-term commitment and will tend to concentrate on approaches that will make it easier for them to do their jobs while at the same time perpetuating themselves. Thus, it is unlikely that labor-saving techniques will be introduced. Computers are fine, but larger classes should be avoided.

The above description has been valid until recent years. Conditions, however, are beginning to change, and in some cases rapidly. Universities can no longer depend upon their sources of revenue being large enough to meet their costs. As losses have developed, private universities have turned to raising their prices, that is, tuition. In turn, because public universities have continued to be heavily subsidized, private universities have had to look for ways of reducing their costs in order to keep from pricing themselves out of the market. Hospitals are moving into much the same position. Because of increasing operating costs and the resulting increased cost of hospitalization insurance to the public, hospitals have been subjected to pressure to operate more efficiently. Governments have looked toward the reduction of expenditures because of heavy pressure against high taxes. As a result of the pressure on gifts and taxes, many nonprofits have begun to find ways to help themselves. There has been over the last five years a significant increase in the fees already charged, such as tuition, hospital charges, admission fees, and similar types of "prices." Furthermore, new fees have been placed on services that were formerly free. The most dramatic change has been in revenues derived from profit-making ventures (see *Newsweek*, January 5, 1987, pp. 38–39, for a number of examples). Many nonprofits of different kinds are engaging in commercial ventures to supplement their revenues. The effect will be to make each of the organizations become better managed as they are forced to search for cost reductions as well as new sources of revenue.

Thus, we see currently in nonprofits a drive to decrease costs. In a profit-making organization, where the revenue source is most directly related to the market system, firms worry about ways of increasing revenue as well as ways of decreasing costs. As I argued earlier, however, because the sources of revenue for nonprofits are not as closely related to performance as in businesses, part of the pressure for improved management that exists in profit-making organizations is absent in nonprofit organizations.

The lack of managerial innovations should not be interpreted as meaning that nonprofits do not innovate in areas related to their program objectives (Young 1983, pp. 127–131). On the contrary, nonprofits, particularly universities, have been engaged in research that has become the basis for product and process innovation in industries. Nonprofits have been actively innovating in their own programs, with many new ideas among arts organizations and human service organizations.

ALLOCATION OF FINANCIAL RESOURCES WITHIN NONPROFIT ORGANIZATIONS

One of the critical functions within an organization is the allocation of resources, which determines the character of the organization. Those activities receiving resources are elected to live and function within the organization; depending upon the amount of resources available in relation to need, such activities may prosper or merely survive. Yet little has been done to develop proper techniques to guide the manager of the nonprofit organization in making resource allocations. This condition is not unique to nonprofits. For resource allocation to particular areas such as advertising and research and development, the business firm devises arbitrary rules to guide itself in lieu of specific market criteria. Frequently these rules of thumb involve an allocation based on some percentage of sales (Baumol and Quandt 1964; Simon 1959).

The problem of allocation is handled effectively and objectively for the economic system as a whole through prices. The beauty of the price system is that resources are allocated in the economy through the dollar votes of consumers. Except for the government sector, resources are allocated without the intervention of individuals. In other words, within the economy we have developed a system of resource allocation that is objective and that represents the goals of the participants of the organization. I am not arguing that the price system is necessarily indicative of some method of allocating resources that achieves someone's concept of equity, but rather that the price system, given the income distribution of the society, allocates resources objectively and in accord with the preferences of the participants in the organization (that is, the whole society) as measured by their dollar votes.

Within academic organizations resource allocation tends to be made on a historical basis, though student choice may affect this occasionally. In other words, budget allocations tend to be made to each unit on the basis of the unit's previous allocation, taking into account changes in the total resources available for allocation. Thus, the tendency is for the organization to do next year what it is doing this year.

There are a variety of devices designed to shake the organization out of this approach. Sometimes all but a given decrement, say 10 percent of the previous year's budget, is allocated to the unit, and the manager of the unit must then make an argument as to why he should get additional funds. Presumably, those managers making the best argument will get the largest increment. Another device is to require an examination each year of the total amount that the unit needs by forcing it to make an argument annually for its existence.

All of these devices, however, suffer from the fact that no systematic framework exists for the evaluation of the quality of the arguments. In a profit-making organization the rationale can always be an increase in profits. In a nonprofit organization arguments for an increased allocation have to be made in terms of increasing the quality of the services offered and/or increasing the variety of services offered. The organization must then make the decision as to whether that improvement in quality and/or that increase in the variety of services is desired, given the total resources available.

In the absence of any objective criteria, such as prices or profits, the allocation of resources within the organization will tend to be based on a political process. In a university, for example, those deans who are most articulate may be able to influence the president or the budget officer to allocate a larger proportion of funds to their units. In other words, the missing element in making resource allocation rational is the discipline and objectivity of a price system. There exist no methods for making measurements on a comparable basis, such as the increase to profit from certain allocations.

The lack of a systematic basis for resource allocation results from the absence of a well-specified set of goals for the organization. Without a clear understanding within the organization of a set of goals and a set of priorities designed to implement those goals, there will always be ambiguity and arbitrariness in the resource allocation process. It is clear that the nonprofit organization must develop a set of goals and allocate resources in accordance with it. The goals will then function as preferences that are determined under a price system by dollar voting, and resources can be allocated on a rational basis.

Developing a set of goals is difficult for any organization, but particularly for a nonprofit, where there is generally great disparity among the members. As a result, consensus on goals is not easily achieved. There are frequent discussions in textbooks about the need for the organization to have goals, but little work has been done to describe a process by which these goals may be determined (Likert 1959). It is clear that the set of goals must simulate the dollar voting process represented by the price system. There does not need to be actual voting, but all of the relevant constituencies in the organization must have a chance to participate in the determination of the organization's goals. The key, however, is that someone in the organization—in my view, the top management—must attempt to pull together the various inputs from the organization's constituencies and develop a comprehensive set of goals as well as the priorities inferred from these goals. There can be many approaches to this process. One that was tried for a university is described below.

The process started with planning at the grass-roots level. Within a university this means planning at the departmental level. The central administration provided some guidelines concerning the nature of the planning process. An emphasis was put on actively involving all of the individual faculty members in the planning process and the need to develop a strategy to achieve the goals of the individual unit. The central administration also indicated to the departments and other planning units the special considerations with which it wanted the planning activity to be concerned. Specifically, the central administration wanted each department and college to determine those areas in which it has a natural comparative advantage because of location, individuals at the school, tradition, or particular strengths in the departments or related areas. The administration provided a broad analysis of the environment in which the organization was expected to operate. Each department, however, developed its own goals and a strategy for achieving those goals. The goals were then analyzed at the college level, where further refinements were made, and intercollege and interdepartment goals were developed. The nonacademic units developed a set of goals in a similar fashion.

All of these individual units went through the discipline of discussing and defending their documents before a centrally organized policy body which the president chaired. After all the individual plans were discussed and defended, the president made a first draft of the set of goals for the organization and developed at the same time a set of priorities for implementing the goals. The document was then given to all the relevant constituencies in the organization. Within the university these are trustees, faculty, students, and alumni. Within some organizations there may be other constituencies, and within some colleges certain of these constituencies may not be relevant. Each of the constituencies should have an organized process by which the goals document is discussed. Well-described channels should be developed for getting feedback on the recommended changes to the president. In other words, there must be a process by which each of the constituencies gives its reactions and suggested modifications of the goals and priorities. The president must then take into account these inputs and develop a document that is consistent with his or her concept of the organization's goals, but one that does represent a workable consensus for the organization.

The process is a cumbersome one, but is designed to reduce the arbitrariness with which resources tend to be allocated within an organization, and is designed to bring greater unity to the organization through participation by its relevant constituencies. The ultimate success of the process will depend upon the ability of the president to find those areas of consensus and relate them to those objectives he or she believes are important to the organization.

BUDGETING IN NONPROFIT ORGANIZATIONS

The most common procedure for budgeting in nonprofit organizations is to begin with the expense side. The position seems to be one of attempting to determine the amount of expenditure that is necessary for the organization in the coming year. Budget forms are sent to the units of the organization that are authorized to make expenditures. Suggested guidelines on the desired limits to expenditures are generally given in the form of some percentage, such as "salary increases should not exceed 4 percent of last year." The attempt of the guidelines is to keep some control on expenditures.

However, it is well known, both in budgeting and organization theory, that the budgeting process is one that can be described in game theory terms (Charnes and Stedry 1964). The unit preparing a budget recognizes that management will cut the proposed budget by some amount. Therefore, the tendency is to incorporate this knowledge in the budget and increase the proposed expenditures by something more than the expected cut. When the cut is made the unit will still have the funds that it desires. The net result of this process is that invariably budgets are submitted at a level higher than management desires. The usual procedure then is to iterate the process. Management cuts the individual budgets, usually at some conference with the managers of the individual units, and new budgets are submitted. Unfortunately, this process takes a great deal of time and leaves the budget for the coming period in a somewhat ambiguous state. Frequently, as for example in universities, commitments for the coming year have to be made before the budget, handled in this fashion, is settled. Thus, management will be confronted after some time with the argument that the unit can no longer cut its budget because commitments have already been made.

In a period when revenues are increasing and, perhaps, expansion is expected in organizations, such a process may well be a viable one. In fact, incentives to get increased funds may well result in the individual units developing some innovative ideas to justify increased budget allocations. The process is unsatisfactory, however, during a period when the organization is contracting or when revenues are expected at best to remain constant. In those circumstances a tighter rein must be kept on the budgeting process, and management cannot afford a large number of iterations with the concomitant commitments that will prevent budget decreases.

An alternative and more acceptable procedure is to begin the budgeting process from the revenue side. Revenue estimates for the budget period are made by the appropriate central management unit in the organization. These estimates will become a guiding force in the budgeting process. The difficulty with this approach, aside from the technical problems of making forecasts, is the tendency to bias revenue estimates in a downward direction (Cyert and March 1963, pp. 67–82). This biasing tendency derives from the fact that the estimating unit has a biased payoff matrix. The estimating unit will clearly suffer more criticism and other forms of negative reprisals if its estimates turn out to be too optimistic. The organization may run a deficit because it based its budgeting process on overly optimistic revenue estimates. Conversely, there will generally be little negative feedback to the unit if the actual revenue turns out to be greater than the estimated revenue and the organization ends the budgeting period with a surplus. Therefore, the estimates must be examined closely to eliminate the tendency toward downward biasing. It is also important that rewards be given for accuracy in the estimates and that underestimation as well as overestimation be criticized.

Once the revenue estimates are made and refined, it is then possible to begin the second step in the budgeting process, which is to make actual allocations of the revenue to the operating units. It is at this point that the objectives and priorities for the organization come into play. As was indicated earlier, the objectives become the preference system made apparent by expenditures for an economy using the price system for allocating resources. It is on the basis of the objectives that the allocation of dollars is made to the units. At the same time, it is clearly difficult to get objectives so specific that they can be translated into precise dollar terms. It is possible to develop an ordering of objectives that can be translated into the relative size of the allocations to the various units, and this is the process that should be followed in determining the dollar allocations for the operating units. It is desirable, however, to have the participation of the managers of the units before the precise amounts for each unit are finalized. It is also important, however, that the first attempt at allocation be made by the top management group. After the participation of the operating managers, the allocations are made within the constraint of the total revenue estimate. A third step in the process can then begin: the detailed determination of the individual budgets by unit. In contrast, however, to the previous process, each manager knows the total dollar amount that the budget must equal. Thus, the unit managers have the freedom to allocate the dollars that they have been given within their own units in the fashion they believe will come closest to achieving the objectives of their units. The top management can rest comfortable because it knows that the budgets, when they are submitted, will be consistent with the best estimates of revenue available.

This process leads to faster completion of the budget cycle because it eliminates the various iterations. At the end of the process the budget is balanced, in surplus, or in deficit, depending upon the target the top management had at the time the revenue was allocated. Success in terms of reaching the target is dependent upon the quality of the revenue estimates and the quality of the control mechanisms within the organization. One additional factor might be noted on the problem of achieving targets. Every organization is in an environment that it cannot completely control. This means that there will be variance on both the revenue and expenditure sides. Study should be made of the past relationship between the estimates and the actuals with respect to revenue and between the budgeted expenditures and the actual expenditures for the individual units. Statistical calculations of the variance can be made, and a contingency reserve can be built into the budget that will protect the unit against missing its target some given proportion of the time. Thus, it may be possible, for example, on the basis of the calculations of the variance, to determine the amount that is necessary to protect against a deficit 95 percent of the time. Such built-in contingencies, of course, do reduce the amounts of money available for allocation. Over time, however, such a reserve may be developed to serve as a cushion to protect against the fluctuations in the actual operating budget.

LONG-RANGE BUDGETING

Despite the difficulties of making estimates far in advance, it is vital to an organization to budget at least five years in advance. This type of budgeting is important because of the longer period of time it may take the organization to free itself from contractual commitments to individual participants. An obvious example within universities is the multiple-year contract with faculty members. If a university were to decide to reduce the size of its faculty, it would clearly take a number of years to do so because of the varying lengths of the contracts of its faculty. Similarly, if a university decided to abandon a certain program, it would take about four years to execute the decision because of commitments to students already in the program. Thus, only by setting targets in the future can the university attain a different disposition of its resources and move into significantly new kinds of activities.

In order to do long-range budgeting it is obvious that a specific set of goals must be available. Long-range budgeting requires guidelines on the directions that the organization is taking. Such directions can come only from the goals statement. The long-range budget is an attempt to translate goals into a set of monetary requirements for achieving those goals at some definite time.

By applying "backward induction" it is possible to develop a series of operational plans for each of the years (DeGroot 1970, pp. 277–278). For example, let us assume a five-year budget. By specifying the position at which the organization wishes to be five years from now, it is possible to work backward and determine where the organization must be at year four if it is to achieve the goals posited by year five. Similar reasoning applies for years three, two, and one. Each year the budget must be revised in the light of changing environmental conditions and in the light of changing goals. The first year of the five-year plan each year becomes the operating budget for the current year. In this fashion the organization develops a means of directing itself toward particular positions. In the absence of such a budget the tendency is to make decisions on the basis of goals that remain implicit or short-run. By failing to make the goal structure explicit the organization risks working with a goal structure that is inconsistent and, in some cases, perhaps, with goals that can never be achieved. Each decision tends to become ad hoc, and new implicit goals may be developed for the purpose of making a decision in an easier fashion (Wolf 1984, pp. 68–112). Furthermore, when the organization changes personnel the new decision-makers have great difficulty understanding past decisions, and the ability to maintain continuity in the organizational strategy is destroyed.

The form of the budget is not as critical in the development of the objectives of the organization as the effort to plan for the achievement of the objectives. There has been in recent years great emphasis on PPBS—Planning Programming Budgeting System—made popular by the Defense Department under Secretary Robert McNamara. The virtue of PPBS is to focus the organization's attention on the specific programs within the organization without regard to the organizational units. But the real virtue of PPBS is that management is forced to examine the objectives of individual programs. Such an examination helps make organizational managers more conscious of the direction in which they are heading. However, program goals are better developed as part of the total goal structure, and I have discussed one method for developing overall objectives for the organization. When budgeting falls naturally into programs it can be developed along PPBS lines. In general, a major objective statement accomplishes most of the good things contributed by PPBS and may be cheaper and more practical to implement. Nevertheless, PPBS has called attention to the importance of programs that are not within the traditional organizational boundaries, and it is critical for universities in particular to develop interdisciplinary programs. Where the development of such activities can be helped by program budgeting, then program budgeting should be used. The more general point is that the overall objectives of the organization are critical for long-range budgeting, and the individual program objectives are significant only against that background.

CONCLUSION

This chapter has developed some of the issues involved in nonprofit management. It should be clear that generic management education is favored. The concept of broad general management for managers in any field is the correct position, in my view. However, it is certainly also clear that there are some institutional differences between the various nonprofit organizations and businesses. Therefore, some material is needed in the curriculum for nonprofit management that emphasizes institutional differences. There is also a need to specify more clearly the differences that a manager faces in a nonprofit organization. The whole question, for example, of volunteers in certain nonprofits is something that generally does not face a business manager. There are differences of this kind, and attention should be paid to some of them. In many cases, however, general management principles will give enough background so that an individual nonprofit manager can deal with these issues.

The optimum curriculum is one that stresses general management principles but contains some courses that have specificity with respect to different fields. I believe that it is clear that universities, the arts, and hospitals each have institutional peculiarities to which some attention should be paid. However, such attention should not be concentrated on institutional peculiarities but on general principles. We must, above all, educate people in management so that the individuals are good managers. The more help we can give them on institutional peculiarities, the better they will be in the long run.

The alternative to this approach is to educate managers for specific nonprofits. Programs would be needed for educational administrators, hospital administrators, foundation executives, museum heads, and so on. Clearly, there would have to be in each one of these curricula a large number of courses that would be the same. Every course dealing with a methodology such as accounting or strategic planning or with an aspect of society such as economics would be common across the curricula. Therefore, the notion of having completely separate curricula does not make economic sense except for a university that has a large student body in each area. Separate sections of the same course might then be justified.

But the other danger that must be faced is the wasting of the students' time by teaching the details of a particular type of nonprofit when those details can be more easily learned on the job. Thus, the student who is well educated in management should be in a position to run any type of nonprofit. He or she should be taught in school a methodology for learning and understanding the peculiarities of the particular type of nonprofit as well as the peculiarities of the particular organization. The methodology is appropriate for the classroom; descriptive detail is not. The education should be broad enough and deep enough to allow the student to transfer his or her knowledge across types of nonprofits as well as organizations.

One of the most important questions about nonprofit management is where curriculum should be. There is extremely strong evidence that a program for nonprofit managers should not be in the business school. Even though I have advocated the usage of business school philosophy on management and utilizing a large part of the business school curriculum, it is extremely important to have the curriculum for nonprofit management in another school. A school of public policy or public administration or urban affairs is the proper place for such a program. The evidence is strong that nonprofit management curricula become lost in a business school. If one looks at the future, it is clear that nonprofit institutions are becoming increasingly important in our society (Young 1983, pp. 9–20). Fortunately, more attention is beginning to be given to this area. In terms of the structure of our society, these types of organizations are particularly significant. Many of the most important human services are delivered through these nonprofit organizations. Therefore, it behooves us to pay serious attention to the curriculum and the place in the university to which that curriculum should be assigned.

There are many reasons why a nonprofit program becomes lost in a business school. Perhaps the major reason is the education of the faculty. They have generally studied some aspect of the business firm, and their interests are attuned to the firm. The interest of American students is predominantly in profit-making enterprises. Thus, students interested in a nonprofit management career will be in the minority in a business school. It will be difficult for the school to be as responsive to the interests of the minority as the majority. General discussions with faculty, types of seminar speakers, and outside speakers generally will be slanted, and properly so, toward the majority interest.

Thus, the student will not feel as comfortable, and therefore will probably not learn as much as he or she might in a school devoted to nonprofit management. There is also a good chance that students will be lost from the nonprofit program and transfer to the business programs as they make salary comparisons. While valid, these are not overwhelming reasons to avoid the business school, however.

The best evidence is that those schools involving areas of management other than business have survived best when established outside the business school. The schools of public administration are a good example. The most distinguished schools of this kind are independent of the business school. It is difficult for two programs with motives so different to survive in the same school even though they have many courses in common.

The ideal solution is to have a large enough student body to justify a self-contained curriculum in a school devoted to organizations motivated by objectives unrelated to profit. The already existing schools fitting this category are basically those of public administration. While the government area should not be confused with the nonprofit area, the two are compatible intellectually. Both have a number of management courses in common and could share them without danger of the kind of problems we described in discussing business schools. Similarly, many seminars with outside speakers could be of common interest. Furthermore, nonprofit management could be a field that students in public administration want to learn about in order to broaden their own job prospects.

The school of public policy or administration is generally one that reaches out to other colleges and departments on campus. Thus, it is easy when the nonprofit management program is embedded in such a college to develop ties with the fine arts department or college. Such ties make it possible to develop a good management program that embraces the arts. Other ties, for example with engineering or science departments, could help expand the horizons of the nonprofit management program.

Those of us in universities have an opportunity to make a major contribution to society by educating managers for the nonprofit area. To do so effectively requires imagination and cooperation. These characteristics are not necessarily abundantly supplied in any organization, but it is imperative that we act responsibly to develop quality programs in nonprofit management. Then we must place these programs in colleges that nurture them and develop them into major programs. The objectives are important and demand our best efforts to achieve them.

4

Nonprofit Managers in Different Fields of Service: Managerial Tasks and Management Training

Paul J. DiMaggio

Is there such a thing as nonprofit management? Is there a set of generic skills that managers of nonprofits as diverse as universities, hospitals, art museums, research institutes, agencies for the homeless, day care centers, and dance companies find necessary and sufficient to perform their duties effectively? Or are the problems that confront managers of nonprofits in different fields of service sufficiently diverse to require separate programs of study?

Implicit in these questions is the heroic assumption that students demand management education because of its manifest function—teaching managers how to do things they will need to do—and not because of such latent functions as credentialing, networking, screening, and socialization. My position on this point is that although the manifest and latent functions of management education may diverge, we should at least try to design programs on a technically rational basis, anticipating that our success in doing so will be constrained powerfully by the need to provide latent services that prospective students demand.

With this proviso, we can think of our proximate goal as the discovery of what statisticians refer to as a "clustering solution" to a matrix constituted by rows of managerial positions and columns of task-competency require-

I am grateful to Melissa Middleton and Dennis Young for careful readings and insightful criticisms of earlier drafts. I also benefitted from helpful comments and observations by many persons in attendance at the conference. Support from the National Endowment for the Arts, Research Division, and the Yale Program on Non-Profit Organizations for collection of data on arts administrators reported in this paper is gratefully acknowledged.

ments. In other words, if one divides positions into separate clusters on the basis of the similarity of the skills they require, and if positions that require similar skills are concentrated in specific nonprofit industries, then separate programs are indicated. If there is little clustering of positions by tasks— or if such clusters as exist are widely dispersed across different nonprofit industries—then there is little technical rationale for separate programs.

I shall sidestep the implications of administrative tasks for the vexing issue of whether for-profit and nonprofit management education should take place under the same institutional roof. Instead, I shall largely (but not exclusively) restrict myself to the related question of whether skill requirements cluster at the level of the nonprofit sector as a whole; at the level of nonprofit fields or industries (e.g., health care, education and research, arts and culture, social services); or at even more minute subsectoral levels (nursing homes, but not health; private secondary schools, but not education; dance companies, but not the arts). This last possibility—that variation in the needs of managers may be greater among organizations within nonprofit service areas than between organizations in different areas—is one that must be taken seriously, for, if true, it would be almost as prejudicial to the advocacy of service-area–based specialization as would finding no clustering beneath the nonprofit sector level at all.

Unfortunately, we lack the data base needed to perform the clustering analysis I have suggested. In its absence, I shall simply lay out a framework for thinking about the problem, supplementing my observations with allusion to a few relevant studies and with some findings of my own research on the preparation of top managers of art museums, resident theatres, orchestras, and local arts agencies (DiMaggio 1987).*

I shall start by considering what we know about the skills that nonprofit managers actually employ, and then point to some kinds of variation among nonprofit firms in different fields of service that might be expected to influence the administrative qualifications such firms require. Next, I shall discuss the manner in which managerial career patterns affect nonprofit management education by shaping both the students to be trained and the expectations of those students about the training they will need. Finally, I shall address several other factors that influence demand for management training (and the kind of training demanded) and make the task of program design more complex than it would be in a thoroughly rational and stable world: the institutionalization in separate fields of service of arbitrarily different language, standard operating procedures, and administrative conventions; the role of management education in the efforts of nonprofit managers

---

*I shall address the universe of charitable nonprofits (501(c)3 operating organizations and independent philanthropic foundations), but not mutual benefit organizations or churches. The focus throughout is on the training of executives as opposed to the education of staff specialists.

to professionalize and affirm their authority; and the tendencies of different skills to cluster at different levels and of change in industry structures to alter both skill requirements and the levels at which they cluster over time.

WHAT DO MANAGERS DO?

There are at least four different views of the role of managers in the literature on organizational behavior. The first is *dramaturgic*: the manager is a leader, a symbol, a cheerleader, a creator of culture, animating his or her employees and conveying with every action the distinctive ethos of the organization and the importance of its mission (e.g., Barnard 1938). A second perspective (described in but not advocated by Abernathy and Hayes 1980) is *technocratic*, viewing the administrator as master technician, who by designing budgets, management information systems, and incentive plans, sets the course of an organization that can then more or less run itself. A third view is *strategic*. Administrators, it is said, manage not the organization itself, but the organization's environment, representing their firm to clients and regulators, developing competitive plans, and raising funds (Pfeffer and Salancik 1978). Yet another perspective is *pragmatic*, viewing the manager as a handyman who puts out fires and takes on critical problems as they unexpectedly arise (Cyert and March 1963; Mintzberg 1973).

These perspectives bear different implications for management education. The dramaturgic view implies that students, if they do not actually possess charisma, must develop powerful communicative skills, perhaps by combining courses in theatre arts and symbolic anthropology. Intrinsic to the technocratic position is faith in the supreme importance of the generalist analytic and management skills that business schools teach. (How else could one justify educating under the same roof managers of firms that, respectively, print newspapers, process steel, bake bread, write software, rent automobiles, and offer health services?) The environmental perspective has perhaps the greatest affinity with specialized curricula, because of the diversity of environments that organizations face, and commends the importance of training in politics and policy. The "handyman" image suggests the need for knowledge that is deep and organization-specific, but perhaps not very broad, and resonates with the protestations of many nonprofit managers that they have done their most important learning on the job.

The handyman model is the least glamorous, but it is also the one best supported by the few empirical studies of what nonprofit executives actually do. In one of the best such studies, Michael Cohen and James March (1974, p. 203) describe the college president as

a bit like the driver of a skidding automobile. The marginal judgments he makes, his skill, and his luck may possibly make some difference to the survival prospects for his riders. As a result, his responsibilities are heavy. But whether he is convicted of manslaughter or receives a medal for heroism is largely outside his control.

According to Cohen and March, all of the diverse set of presidents they studied worked long hours, found the job "physically and emotionally exhausting," and experienced chronic frustration at "being unable to attend adequately to the 'important' aspects of their jobs." Presidents spent half their work time on campus, one-sixth at home, one-seventh away from campus but in town, and more than one-fifth on the road. They passed seven or eight hours daily in conversations that, in most cases, they had not initiated.

A prominent museum director describes members of that profession as "beleaguered" by social forces that "squeeze relentlessly from all sides," buffeted from encounter to encounter with trustees, artists, representatives of staff and community and, at the same time, subject to the "necessity of pursuing at least some serious scholarly work to avoid the disdain of academic art historians, the obligations of a frantic social schedule, and the requirement of participating in endless committee meetings" (Leavitt 1972, p. 98). One of his peers characterizes the directorship as combining the roles of "art historian and connoisseur, businessperson and fundraiser, diplomat, politician, lobbyist, personnel manager, publisher, architectural consultant, restaurateur, educator, after-dinner speaker and . . . resident psychoanalyst" (Shestack 1978, p. 27).

According to a recent study (Odendahl, Boris, and Daniels 1985), foundation executives express high levels of satisfaction with their jobs, valuing especially their flexibility and autonomy. Nonetheless, their days are no less full than those of other nonprofit administrators. Most interviewees reported working more than fifty hours a week, dividing their time among such chores as correspondence, reviewing proposals, monitoring projects, brokering support for programs they favor, and engaging in a range of social and ceremonial activities related to the public presence of their institution.

I suspect that these accounts of nonprofit managerial positions in universities, art museums, and foundations would not seem alien to administrators of social service agencies or hospitals. In all of these organizations, top managers are subjected to multiple demands on their time, externally imposed deadlines, and crises that divert them from planning, reflection, and the design of management systems.

Such harassing conditions are doubtless common to the management of many proprietary concerns as well. But they may press harder on nonprofit managers as a group because of the ambiguity and diversity of most nonprofits' goals. One result of the variety of legitimate goals that any nonprofit organization can address, and the absence of bottom-line criteria for effectiveness, is that, compared to proprietary firms, there are probably more plausible courses of action an organization may take, and thus more need for managers to consult with trustees (who, at any rate, are ordinarily a more active, if not more menacing, presence than for-profit directors) and staff about a wider range of decisions. Another is that each possible goal usually has its own external constituencies, often sources of real or potential funding and/or trouble, who demand the manager's attention and time. Moreover, if the manager of a large for-profit has senior staff to whom internal tasks may be delegated while he or she manages the organization's environment, even relatively large nonprofits rarely shield their managers from involvement in day-to-day decisions about everything from physical plant to marketing and labor relations.

HOW DO ORGANIZATIONS DIFFER BY SUBFIELD?

Nonprofit managers must, as a group, cope with the challenges of goal ambiguity, multiple constituencies, and limited staff support (relative the giant enterprises that employ most MBAs). Nonetheless, nonprofit organizations in different fields of service differ in ways that may influence the skills that the administrator needs.

Size

One important differentiating factor is size, which generates managerial problems (visibility and greater constituent and regulatory demands, administrative complexity and coordination requirements, a higher probability of unionization, the need for endowment management, greater capital costs, and more complex physical plant maintenance arrangements) and managerial solutions (the resources to hire administrative staff with specialized expertise) (Blau 1970; for the arts, Peterson 1986). Under a certain size, nonprofits can often be managed by a generalist who knows how to do several things very well, while letting others ride. Above a certain size threshold, the nonprofit executive becomes a different kind of generalist, in need of some familiarity with, but not necessarily expertise in, a wider range of functions and some ability, trained or innate, in the administration of persons.

To what extent does size correlate with field of service? There is some relationship, but not a perfect one. National federated service agencies are, on average, larger than colleges, which are larger than social service agencies, which have larger budgets than day care centers. The typical art museum employs more staff than the average orchestra, which in turn is bigger than most nonprofit theatres. There are no mammoth dance companies and no three-person hospitals. On the other hand, there is substantial size variation within every nonprofit field. And, because the smallest nonprofits may not be able to afford to hire university-trained managers anyway, the implications of size variation for the design of management training programs may be less significant than they appear.

Technology

A source of differentiation more relevant to the focus of this chapter—because it covaries more substantially with field of service—is core technology (Perrow 1967). Indeed, variation in core technology is commonly invoked as a rationale for separate training programs. Different technologies pose different administrative problems. Residential nonprofits like hospitals and nursing homes need managers skilled in labor relations and capable of overseeing functions that, like food purchasing, room scheduling, and maintenance, are often associated with hotel-motel management. By contrast, administrators of performing arts organizations may need different logistical skills in order to schedule tours and negotiate short-term contracts (Peterson 1986).

Related to this is the presumed need for an administrator to have some familiarity with the core technology itself. Art museum directors, for example, are expected to have some grasp of, if not actively to contribute to, art-historical scholarship; hospital administrators to know something about medical care; and university presidents to have some familiarity with research and classroom instruction. Technical training in none of these specialties would be appropriate for a core curriculum in general nonprofit management, and only an exceptionally large management school could provide even occasional electives in such areas (although they could encourage, as many do, use of courses offered by other schools in their universities).

It is, of course, a matter of dispute as to whether an executive need know much more about an organization's core technology than he or she could learn in a relatively short time on the job. (Fewer than half of the arts managers I surveyed believed it important for a prospective executive to be deeply familiar with the art form he or she managed, although large majorities in each field thought it very important that he or she appreciate the art that the organization produced or exhibited [DiMaggio 1987].) Where organizations are highly professionalized, core technical activities (curing, counseling, curating, caring) are delegated to trained specialists, and managers often portray themselves as "facilitators."

At the same time, however, well-organized technical professionals may pursue objectives discrepant from those that managers and trustees favor and may attempt to define nearly every aspect of administration as relevant to their work and thus subject to their professional authority. Under such circumstances, professional managers must learn enough about core technologies to establish control over management functions. This is especially true in organizations—nonprofit or proprietary—that employ plural professionals (doctors and nurses in hospitals, curators and educators in museums), where managers must adjudicate turf disputes among competing professions (Ritti and Goldner 1969; Scott 1983). Thus, even if specialized technical knowledge were unnecessary for the execution of generic managerial duties in consensual organizations, political factors may require it in real ones.

External Environments

If internal differences between nonprofits in different fields of service require that managers possess different skills, variation in the external environment they face may be equally important. Peterson (1986), for example, argues that the transition in the managerial style of executives of museums and performing arts organizations from the entrepreneurial, charismatic impresario to the more conservative, technically skilled, rationalistic arts administrator resulted largely from environmental rather than internal organizational changes.

Revenue sources play a key role in this respect. There is little reason for trustees of a nonprofit social service agency supported *in toto* by public funds to require its executive to be trained in marketing (unless they want to change that situation), and much reason for it to demand political sophistication. By contrast, a youth service organization seeking to cross-subsidize service programs by selling recreational opportunities to the upper middle class, or a theatre dependent for revenues upon its subscription audience, requires (although it may not get [see Hirsch and Davis 1979]) management that is at least familiar with, if not expert in, marketing.

Similarly, the degree and kind of training in human resource management an organization's managers need will depend on whether it is unionized or likely to become so (on differences between unionized and nonunionized nonprofit industries, see Young 1984). It is hard to conceive of a hospital (or, increasingly, a university) board that would not be sensitive to an administrator's background in labor relations, and difficult to imagine many private foundation boards that would even inquire about the topic.

Fields vary in their competitiveness and volatility. Where competition is substantial (e.g., in health care), formal planning skills may be especially vital. Where cooperation is mandated by funding agencies, legislation, or some other external authority (as is often the case, for example, in the social services), political sophistication and the ability to manage joint programs are more important.

Such mandates for cooperation represent an example of regulation; and regulation may be one of the most important sources of differentiation among nonprofits in different fields of service, and perhaps the source that fits most closely with industry boundaries. The health care field, with its myriad regulatory authorities impinging on almost every realm of managerial discretion, is a notable example. But even the art museum director must be conversant with regulations governing the importation of art across national boundaries and IRS rulings defining related and unrelated income. Moreover, executives of nonprofits that are either regulated by or receive substantial resources from government must have some knowledge of and ability to express themselves about public policy issues in their domains.

Specialization in Subfields

Skill requirements may be so highly particular to specific types of non-profit organizations that even specialized programs in health management, arts management, or educational management cannot address the differences adequately. In our surveys of arts managers, some such variations by sub-field appeared when executives were asked to evaluate the importance of several criteria for choosing a top manager of an organization like their own. For example, approximately three-fifths of the theatre managing di-rectors and local arts agency directors regarded "grantsmanship" ability as very important, compared to fewer than half of the orchestra managers and just over one-quarter of the art museum directors. Similarly, just over half of the art museum directors reported that the ability to prepare a budget was very important, compared to more than 80 percent of administrators in each of the other fields (perhaps reflecting the higher level of staff support available to the former). (Notably, fewer than 20 percent in any field thought "formal training in administration" was a "very important" criterion [DiMaggio 1987].)

For-Profit/Nonprofit Differences

Although no one, to my knowledge, has studied differences in the task composition of managerial work in nonprofit and for-profit organizations in the same industry, we may speculate as to whether such organizations differ with respect to factors that might influence managerial tasks. Al-though the modal size of nonprofit and proprietary firms varies within industries, mean differences (at the workplace level) are rarely large, and there is always much within-group variation. Although for-profits in the health and service industries have been faster than nonprofits to adopt multi-unit forms of organization, which pose particular managerial challenges of coordination and control, where for-profit chains have been successful, nonprofit producers are usually forced to compete—either by merging to form chains of their own or by adopting some other approach to aggregating enterprises that poses similar managerial dilemmas.

If in the long run nonprofit firms and their proprietary competitors are likely to become similar in average size and complexity, managerial roles are also unlikely to differ within industries with respect to core technologies. Although proprietaries may avoid certain money-losing tasks, in most in-dustries where for-profit and nonprofit firms coexist, they will include more or less the same mix of professions doing more or less the same kinds of things.

If managers of proprietary and nonprofit organizations in the same business need different skills, the causes will lie outside the firms in their environments (Fottler 1981). The different legal charters of the two forms, to give just one obvious example, prevent nonprofits from distributing a surplus and more or less oblige for-profits to attempt to do so (Hansmann 1980). The implications of this difference for the ways in which for-profits and nonprofits define their goals and evaluate both personnel and programs are considerable.

Moreover, in many industries, the nonprofit manager must be prepared to deal with a range of publics and granting authorities, whereas the proprietary manager must worry more about financial control and pricing decisions. If the nonprofit executive has recourse to certain resources—volunteer services and foundation grants, for example—that his or her proprietary counterpart does not, he or she must also be prepared to satisfy and respond to a larger and somewhat different set of external constituencies (Kramer 1985a). One may generalize by suggesting that the for-profit manager must understand economics, whereas the nonprofit manager must have a strong intuitive grasp of politics (with the understanding that each will be better off if he or she is adept at both).

Obviously, the extent to which nonprofit and proprietary environments differ varies from industry to industry as a function of state policy and the intra-industry division of labor. Where government supports a service by funding clients or by contracting to both for-profits and nonprofits, and where the state's zeal for regulating firms in both sectors is constant, the tasks of nonprofit and for-profit executives will be more similar than where the opposite is the case. Where nonprofits and proprietaries compete directly, nonprofit managers will find that they need the economic skills necessary to meet the competition (see, e.g., Skloot 1987). (This seems to be occurring in the hospital industry, where competition drives nonprofits and for-profits ever closer in structure and administrative style.) Where nonprofit and for-profit firms occupy distinct niches—as in the field, for example, of postsecondary education, where nonprofits tend to provide multiyear courses of study culminating in the acquisition of formal credentials and for-profits sell specific technical courses—environments and thus managerial skill requirements are likely to differ very sharply.

CAREERS

What prospective students expect of management education is doubtless influenced by their career experiences and career expectations. Management students do not arrive on campus freshly hatched out of eggs. Frequently, they bring to their education substantial amounts of experience in the fields they will manage.

The extent to which this is the case varies from field to field, of course.

About half of the arts executives we surveyed majored as undergraduates in the artistic disciplines they would oversee, and from just over 40 percent of the arts agency directors and orchestra managers to over 80 percent of the arm museum directors had relevant aesthetic graduate training as well. Most of the younger art museum directors had taught art history at universities, and most of the older ones had served as curators. Almost half of the theatre managing directors had worked as actors, artistic directors, or technical staff before becoming administrators. Artistic experience was also common among the arts agency and orchestra managers.

What these executives lacked was not experience in the fields that they would administer, but rather experience in administration. When asked about the quality of their preparation for a range of management functions (fiscal management, personnel management, board relations, planning and development, marketing and public relations, labor relations, and government relations), fewer than half of the theatre managing directors, art museum directors, or orchestra managers described themselves as well prepared for any of these functions upon taking their first executive post. (Local arts agency directors, who were somewhat more likely to have attended management courses or to have had other kinds of nonprofit management experience, were only somewhat more buoyant, with small majorities rating their preparation for planning/development and marketing/public relations as good.) Substantial minorities in each field frankly described their preparation for each function as "poor" (DiMaggio 1987). (Regrettably, I am aware of no comparable data from MBA-holding proprietary executives.) One would presume that most, but not all, of these executives had more need for in-service training in generic management skills than for socialization into the mores of their subdisciplines.

Note, however, an irony in this line of reasoning. Were nonprofit management degrees to become prerequisites for entry into these fields, we would probably witness a shift in managerial backgrounds away from artistic and toward administrative expertise. Were this to occur, the case for specialized training might become more compelling.

The art museum directorship is interesting, but not unique, because it often represents a career-culminating reward for a man or woman who has made his or her mark doing something unrelated to administration. The percentage of art museum directors who hold Ph.D.s in art history and the percentage coming from academic backgrounds (neither of which represents evident preparation for administration) has increased throughout the postwar period (DiMaggio 1987). Similarly, the percentage of college and university presidents holding Ph.D.s has risen over the course of this century. Moreover, college and university presidents "have almost exclusively academic experience. . . . Most enter an institution of higher education at about age 18 and except for military service spend the rest of their prepresidential life there" (Cohen and March 1974, pp. 15, 24).

Men and women reaching the college presidency by this route may find their new responsibilities daunting, a reaction reflected in former Yale President Giamatti's recollections (1986) of his first days in office:

I learned about the corporate world. I learned that because the corporate world is only interested in quarterly results, it talks a great deal about long-range planning. It was clear to me that Yale needed some of that too. We needed a corporate strategy, we needed management objectives, we needed goals and incentives to achieve results, we needed a policy. I, of course, had no policies. I had a mortgage and one suit, but no policies. . . . What was it that . . . would most contribute to solving our deficit, enhancing our quality and making me a Manager?

By contrast, executives in some other nonprofit fields arrive at their posts through more idiosyncratic routes, external to the institutions they eventually manage. Odendahl, Boris, and Daniels (1985, chap. 4) report that the foundation executives they studied were recruited from business, universities, other operating nonprofits, and the professions. Despite the diversity of routes, however, the executives were carefully screened—and, one expects, socialized to the nuances of the foundation community if not trained in the skills of administration—due to the fact that they were in most cases known to, and invited to apply by, the trustees of the foundation they headed. Moreover, most "had formed some prior affiliation with the foundation through fundraising, consulting, or serving on a committee that reviews proposals" (Odendahl, Boris, and Daniels 1985, p. 43).

If the experiences that people bring to nonprofit management education shape what they need and expect to get out of it, so do the careers that they anticipate. Several characteristics of nonprofit managerial careers are relevant here. First, whatever the generalizability of administrative skills, in practice there is little evidence that many managers' careers take them across enterprises in different fields of service. Health administrators are unlikely to become university presidents. And university presidents, although they may some day run foundations, are rarely if ever candidates to head social service agencies.

Specialization occurs even within broadly defined fields. Despite the proliferation of arts management programs dedicated to the proposition that a well-trained arts manager can function effectively in a range of settings, and despite obvious similarities in core technologies within the performing arts, the labor markets for administrators of theatres and orchestras are highly segmented. Local arts agencies have drawn management from the performing arts, although the traffic seems one way; and as this young field matures and develops its own administrative cadre even this flow may come to a halt. Art museum directors do not move on to administer natural history museums, nor do we see history museum executives taking over the administration of zoos (DiMaggio 1987). Segmented labor markets breed differentiated careers, which are conducive to differentiated programs of training.

A second characteristic of nonprofit management careers that may bear implications for training is the tendency for aspiring managers to work in different kinds of posts that require different forms of expertise. Like executives in many for-profit industries, aspiring nonprofit managers often enter a field as staff specialists in large organizations where they must do one thing very well; move on to executive positions in small organizations where they must do a little of everything; and, if things go well, ascend to managerial posts in more substantial institutions in which most of their time is spent coordinating the efforts of specialist staff and negotiating the environment (DiMaggio 1987; Odendahl, Boris, and Daniels 1985). Therefore, even if staff positions and executive positions, or small and large organizations, require different kinds of expertise, the same persons must be prepared to work in all of them at various points in their careers.

A final salient characteristic of nonprofit managerial careers is the extent to which they are characterized by blocked mobility. Because most nonprofit organizations are relatively small (compared to the firms that constitute the corporate market for MBAs), career ladders are short, and talented managers may reach the top early in their professional lives. Although universities are relatively large as nonprofits go, Cohen and March (1974) found that the average college president acceded to that position in his or her mid-forties. They note that the presidency is "the best job he has ever had or is ever likely to have. . . . the best opportunity the typical president can expect is an invitation to accept a decent version of administrative semiretirement" (pp. 2, 201–202). The arts are no different. Two-thirds of all orchestra managers, three-quarters of art museum directors, and nine-tenths of theatre managing directors became executives before turning forty (DiMaggio 1987).

Blocked opportunity leads nonprofit managers to leave their fields. Despite the presence of many respondents who were nearing retirement, approximately one-third of the art museum directors, orchestra managers, and theatre managing directors and more than one-half of the local arts agency directors surveyed reported that it was "very" or "somewhat" likely that they would take a position entirely outside of the arts (DiMaggio 1987). If the segmentation of managerial labor markets suggests the logic of separate programs of education, the frequent exodus of nonprofit managers from their fields of endeavor represents a rationale for more general training.

INSTITUTIONALIZATION AS A SOURCE OF DIFFERENTIATION

To this point I have dwelt largely on task-based sources of differentiation in managerial jobs. On balance, the functions that managers in different nonprofit fields must perform are rather similar. To the extent that skill requirements vary, they are likely to do so within fields of service, according to organizational size or subarea. This line of argument militates, albeit with much qualification, toward the conclusion that generic nonprofit management training programs are preferable to specialized ones.

Such a conclusion would be premature. One reason for this is that different fields of nonprofit service tend to be highly institutionalized (DiMaggio and Powell 1983; Scott 1983; Zucker, 1986). That is, they generate their own languages, assumptions, routines, and role expectations, quite aside from differences in their technical base. They also generate patterns of communication among managers and staff of organizations within a field that tend to reinforce these differences in language and taken-for-granted assumptions. The result of this is to create large bodies of tacit knowledge that individuals need in order to operate effectively. Thus, an important function of specialized, preservice programs in fields like theatre management or hospital management, quite aside from the inculcation of technical skills, is the initiation of prospective administrators into the language and lore of the arenas that they will enter.

It may be useful, in this regard, to think of institutionalized differentiation among nonprofit areas of service as a problem of social classification, whereby organizations that have much in common are perceived as symbolically and objectively distinct. Museums and libraries, for example, are similar in their size distribution and have in common the collection and conservation of objects and the use of these objects for purposes of public education. Both museums and libraries require managers capable of overseeing these activities, supervising building maintenance and related services, and maintaining amicable relations with community groups and multiple funding sources. Many early museums were part of libraries, and former librarians were prominent among the pioneers of the museum profession. Yet there is little commerce between the two fields. Their managers are trained in separate institutions and disciplines, belong to separate professional societies, and do things in very different ways. Similarly, the management of arts organizations and of entertainment firms has much in common, but there are few programs that attempt seriously to train administrators for both.

Even though differences among institutionalized fields may be arbitrary or traditional rather than based in functional requirements, they nonetheless pose significant barriers to the migration of administrators and thus, potentially, to general programs of nonprofit management training. Dennis Young (1984) discovered substantial differences in employee compensation plans in different parts of the nonprofit world. Similarly, I suspect that the typical hospital administrator would find a university budget bewildering, while a competent social service agency director might quail before the accounting conventions employed in art museums.

Nonprofit fields have no stranglehold on esoteric jargon or idiosyncratic conventions. Institutional differences are apparent among proprietary industries and government agencies as well, yet they do not prevent business schools from training managers for every sort of corporation or keep public managers from jumping from agency to agency. Yet such institutional differences may be more powerful in nonprofit organizations for two reasons. First, because nonprofits do good and pay poorly, commitment to organizational missions and adherence to local mores is particularly prized. By contrast, no proprietary executive would be branded a traitor for moving from boxes to box springs in search of a larger salary or higher profits. Second, although one can think of many exceptions, nonprofit trustees may be less willing than corporate boards or public executives to ignore the preferences of subordinates (especially professionals) in choosing a new manager. Even where managers are no longer recruited from the professional ranks (as in nonprofit hospitals), professionals may exercise a kind of veto power.

Although insularity may be destructive insofar as managers in one field are kept in ignorance of potentially superior administrative methods in adjacent areas, it will not do to dismiss fieldwide conventions as atavisms to be swept away by general management training. If separate conventions or distinct jargons impede communication across service-area boundaries, they facilitate communication, information transfer, and cooperation within them (and with funding agencies that are themselves specialized as to field of service). As we have seen, managing organizational environments that consist of other organizations is central to the nonprofit manager's task and, for this reason, nonprofit management educators must of necessity acknowledge institutional differences among fields as important constraints on the generality of management training.

Insofar as institutional differences among industries in which nonprofit firms operate stem from variation in the technical core or from the presence of different kinds of professionals, for-profits and nonprofits in an industry may be institutionally similar. Conversely, however, nonprofit and proprietary firms generally belong to separate trade associations, which, if active, may themselves generate institutional differences among firms in the two sectors.

PROFESSIONAL POLITICS

A similar constraint on generalist programs is posed by the intimate relationship between formal management training and the professional aspirations of nonprofit managers. Almost without exception, nonprofit managers refer to their specialties (social service administration, the museum directorship, hospital management) as "professions." Yet this self-characterization is frequently contested, and not without reason. Nonprofit managers do not, like most professionals, have clients; they do not control the market for their services; in most fields they do not maintain codes of ethics; nor do they (as opposed to the organizations they run) offer credible claims of disinterested public service. To confuse matters more, many nonprofit executives are members of other professions (librarians, teachers, social workers, scholars) that are distinctly nonmanagerial (Freidson 1986; Majone 1980). Why, then, do they claim, as managers, separate professional status?

In point of fact, nonprofit managers are what Magali Sarfatti Larson (1977) has termed "technobureaucratic professionals"—professionals whose authority rests in their occupancy of administrative positions in bureaucracies and their claims to possession of technical expertise in administration. But if the technobureaucratic professional's authority rests on a claim to administrative expertise, the nature and content of that expertise is far from obvious. Professional knowledge, to represent an effective claim to authority, must be at least partially codifiable, monopolized, acquirable through formal education, and sufficiently tacit to require a combination of both apprenticeship and rote learning (Larson 1977). Managerial knowledge, by contrast, is poorly defined, widely dispersed, and commonly viewed as experiential.

Nonprofit managers are nonetheless compelled to claim professional status for reasons that have more to do with organizational politics than with personal vanity. Although they sit atop organization charts, they are administrators, not czars. Hedged, on the one side, by boards of trustees and, on the other, by technical professionals, the nonprofit manager often finds it difficult to carve out a zone of autonomy and influence. Scott (1983, p. 100) has noted that hospitals employ more than one hundred professional, technical, or vocational specialties,

and the great majority of these are licensed, certified, registered, or in other ways regulated and authorized. . . . once it is determined that a given service is to be offered, administrators exercise relatively little control over what types of occupational groups are to be hired, how work is to be divided among them, or what work routines they are to follow.

Similarly, universities are confederations of professional bailiwicks, each commanding a small part of a differentiated body of knowledge (Freidson 1986). Multiple professionals place multiple constraints on managers. As a museum executive wrote almost seventy years ago, "The director has no rights, but it is customary to allow him certain privileges and the curators will see that these are not abused" (Lucas, quoted in Coleman 1939, p. 404; see also Zolberg 1986).

Even the administrator who comes up through the professional ranks may face loss of prestige among his or her former peers as a result of abandoning professional practice (Goldner and Ritti 1967). And if such managers are, by and large, better able to navigate among their staff than are outsiders to the field, they may find the need to justify their administrative abilities to trustees even greater. An experienced museum administrator has noted:

The prestige of professional status offsets the trustees' perceived affluence and social position. Some museum staff may even fancy that by framing certain issues as "professional" they can reserve the decisions about those issues to themselves. (Weil 1986)

The implications of such internal political considerations for management training revolve around the inescapable fact that management education programs must do double duty, imparting both usable skills and, equally important, formal credentials upon which can be based credible claims of specialized expertise and competence, without which the nonprofit manager will find it difficult to assert his or her authority relative to that of trustees and professional staff. One result is that nonprofit managers will, in general, prefer credential-giving programs to those that offer training but no credentials, independent of the content of instruction that such programs offer.

A second implication is that the choice of location for programs of management training is a political as well as a technical decision. Differentiated programs lodged in schools of social work, education, public health, or art permit managers to define their function as one of several "professional specialties," recognized and credentialed by the same institutions that justify the professional claims of technical or service-providing staff, and, moreover, to acquire a familiarity with the services they will manage and the institutional milieux over which they will preside that cannot be lightly dismissed. By contrast, training in an MBA curriculum permits the nonprofit manager facilely to employ technical terms and techniques that baffle trustees and staff alike and to bask in the halo of the purportedly more efficient proprietary sector. By contrast, generalized training in nonprofit management programs offers neither of these advantages.*

CONFOUNDING PROBLEMS

If technical skill requirements of nonprofit managers' jobs militate toward the use of generic nonprofit management programs, whereas institutional and political factors recommend differentiated programs, other considerations suggest that neither format is likely to be entirely satisfactory. First,

*Having specialized nonprofit tracks within larger MBA-granting institutions would address this problem; however, such programs, if they were to provide useful training, would have to compete successfully for institutional resources with such staples of business education as finance and operations research. The record, where this has been attempted, has not been encouraging.

different skills may cluster at different levels, making general training appropriate for some management functions but specialized training crucial for others. Managers of diverse kinds of nonprofits may benefit from the same courses in accounting, organizational behavior, and human resources development, but need quite different skills in labor relations, board management, or program-related areas. For example, theatre managing directors reported that courses they had taken at business schools provided useful training in personnel management and planning, and rated courses taken in arts administration programs less favorably in this regard. On the other hand, they awarded arts administration programs somewhat higher ratings than general management curricula with respect to courses in marketing and public relations (DiMaggio 1987).

Second, nonprofit industries change in ways that make new skills salient and old ones obsolete. The emergence of specialized organizational forms (nursing homes, hospices, home-care providers, HMOs) in health care has raised dilemmas for programs of hospital management, while increases in competition have given a salience to the marketing function for university and museum administrators that traditional museology and education school programs have been ill equipped to address. Increased differentiation among some nonprofits may create subsectoral needs for new differentiated skills at the same time that increased concentration and competition render many nonprofit administrative roles more similar to one another and to the skills required by managers of proprietary enterprises as well.

CONCLUSIONS

As is by now evident, an examination of the competencies required by nonprofit executives generates persuasive arguments on behalf of both general and specialized nonprofit management training, and insufficient evidence to evaluate these arguments except conjecturally. There are many skill requirements that administrative positions in different fields of service hold in common. General programs in nonprofit management (or even the training of nonprofit managers in general management curricula) may achieve substantial economies of scale with respect to these skills. And our uncertainty about what nonprofit managers really need to know and the tendency for the boundaries of fields and the knowledge their administrators require to change with time militate toward general programs, which, if nothing else, are likely to offer greater flexibility than smaller, more specialized curricula. At the same time, institutional and political factors and the segmentation of labor markets all press toward differentiation.

Moreover, even within a nonprofit field, different students have different needs. Mid-career technical professionals entering managerial positions may benefit most from general management training, while neophytes or man-

agers desirous of crossing over to new nonprofit domains require socialization and field-specific knowledge and networks.

I have not addressed one common argument for specialized programs:
that they sensitize students to the missions of nonprofit organizations as
general management programs cannot. Although this may be a good reason
to keep potential nonprofit executives out of the free-market ideological
cauldrons that many business schools have become, it strikes me as irrelevant
to the choice of general versus specialized training within nonprofit management education itself. For one thing, any manager entering a new nonprofit field will be immediately subject to a vast and unremitting array of
social-psychological forces calculated to enlist his or her commitment to
and identification with the mission of the organization in question and the
values of the field. Without countervailing support from within the organization and its immediate environment, only the most hardened sociopath
could resist these pressures. Given this, there may be more to be said for
the introduction of unorthodox perspectives through hiring generalists than
for the systematic reinforcement of the status quo by hiring only managers
socialized in advance to the field's norms.

Moreover, this concern may credit formal educational programs with
more influence than they have. Management trainees are probably shaped
more by prior work and educational experiences and by their preexisting
value orientations than by anything that happens to them in the course of
a two-year graduate program. If some nonprofit organizations hire managers who are unsympathetic to the goals and ethos of professional staff,
the reason more likely lies in the intentions of trustees (who eventually get
more or less the managers they want) and in the competitive and bureaucratic pressures exerted by the environment than in the training of the
administrators who represent the proximate source of irritation. (Even without controlling for selection effects of this kind, I found formal management
training to be related to market as opposed to product orientation among
theatre managing directors but not among executives of orchestras or local
arts agencies [DiMaggio 1987].)

Nonetheless, quite apart from this concern with mission, familiarity with
the institutional peculiarities of different fields of service is a prerequisite
for effective performance. Consequently, were general management courses
to become the principal port of entry into administration in a given field
(especially one in which managers reach executive positions relatively
quickly), the paradoxical effect would be to generate a legitimate demand
for more specialized training, just as dissatisfaction with the perceived insularity or amateurishness of specialized programs produces calls for comprehensive training in generic skills.

It might be surmised that the best solution would be to create nonprofit
general management programs at large universities wherein students could
supplement their generalized management training with sector-specific

courses in professional schools. But just as the demand-side politics of professional credentialing may make such an alternative unappealing to some prospective students, so the supply-side politics of intrauniversity coordination often cause well-intended efforts at coordination to flounder on the inability of separate units to agree on terms of trade.

All this leads to a banal but inevitable conclusion: the solution, such as it is, lies in the preservation and cultivation of flexibility and diversity. It is my impression that most programs of nonprofit management tend to specialize more than their titles let on. We have "general" programs that largely train social service administrators, "arts management" programs that have placed few if any students on orchestra staffs but whose graduates populate state and local arts agencies, and a range of other creative adaptations that are as functional as they are disingenuous.

At the risk of concluding with a call for more research, I would suggest that synoptic efforts to define the proper form of nonprofit management education risk overlooking the fact that universities and management schools are themselves (private and public) nonprofit institutions, managed by technical professionals with a firm command of their scholarly specialties but relatively little experience or formal training in nonprofit administration, and populated by other technical professionals who will try to adapt any new program to their own practical and intellectual tastes and agendas. It therefore may be useful to train our research focus on the processes by which programs to educate nonprofit managers develop and curricula emerge, with the goal of better understanding the organizational factors that are likely to shape the enterprise in which we are engaged.

5

The Practical Differences in Managing Nonprofits: A Practitioner's Perspective

Bruce C. Vladeck

That most unremittingly logical of political philosophers, Thomas Hobbes (1651, Introduction), argued that the best approach to social analysis was introspection. While Hobbes's methodological opinions have tended to fall out of favor in our ostensibly more modern era, my assignment leaves me little alternative. As a practicing manager of a nonprofit organization, seven years removed from the academic world, and perhaps twice as far removed from any illusion of currency with the professional literature, my only choice is to address what I know, while perhaps trying to put it into somewhat larger perspective.

I have organized my observations and expressed prejudices under five broad headings: governance, planning, finances, human resources, and leadership. Given the methodology of my approach, however, it is necessary to precede that discussion with a few autobiographical statements, as well as some clarification of assumptions.

The United Hospital Fund of New York is a 107-year-old federated charity, created initially by the trustees of some of New York City's leading voluntary hospitals to engage in joint fundraising and charitable distribution, and to carry out related activities of benefit to those institutions and the communities they serve. As it has evolved, the fund is increasingly engaged in research, education, publication, and policy development activities.

The fund is governed by a board of directors, currently comprising twenty-three members, elected to fixed terms by the members of the corporation on nomination by the board. The chairman of the board is, by bylaw, the fund's chief executive officer; the president, according to the same bylaws, is the senior salaried staff member and chief administrative officer. Since 1983 the president has also automatically occupied a seat on the board.

The United Hospital Fund has a current operating budget of roughly $4.2 million and a separate charitable distribution budget of approximately $6.5 million. It employs sixty-two people. About half the operating budget is derived from income on endowment; another quarter from reimbursement of costs associated with the fundraising, United Way, and distribution functions; and the balance from programmatic revenues.

The United Hospital Fund is thus both a grant-maker and a grant-seeker. It is a membership organization but not formally a representative one. It is, as far as we can tell, the only organization of its kind—something that might have some influence on the generalizability of all that is to follow.

The current popularity of the notion of treating nonprofits generically, as reflected not only in this volume but in the creation of organizations and clearinghouses, of which we ourselves belong to at least three, in the context of the topic of this chapter and the uniqueness of my own organization, requires making several assumptions explicit at the outset. I do not believe that all nonprofits are alike in most critical ways, but the discussion here will essentially assume that they are, unless otherwise noted. This chapter will focus primarily on nonprofits in the health and human services sector, because that is most of what I know about, although anyone who thinks my observations may be generalized to other sorts of nonprofits should feel free to do so. I will also largely ignore, except where otherwise explicitly noted, the enormous differences in size and scope among nonprofit organizations even within the same sector, although these differences in scale are quite likely more consequential for management than differences between similarly sized nonprofits and for-profits.

GOVERNANCE

In the context of everything above, it seems to me that the most important difference between nonprofits and other kinds of organizations, from the perspective of day-to-day management, lies in the issues of governance and accountability. My own experience, before I came to the nonprofit sector, was not in the private sector but in government, and the contrast is especially illuminating. The formal organization chart of the New Jersey State Department of Health had at its top not the commissioner, who was two lines down, nor even the governor, who was one line down, but rather, in large letters uncontained in any box, "The People of the State of New Jersey." Granted a certain degree of pretentiousness, if not silliness, in that presentation, the table of organization reflected not only the underlying theoretical flow of authority, but also a useful continuing reminder to all of us as to just who it was we were supposed to be working for.

In any governmental environment I have ever observed, the most basic status distinction is between those officials who are elected and those who are appointed. No matter how inferior in expertise, attention span, intelligence, or even interest level the elected officials might be, the mores of the system legitimately confer on their roles a very special kind of status for which there can be no substitute.

In government, once one gets below the level of elected officials, the lines of authority are very clear. In theory, and to a surprising degree in practice, every official's realm of action is circumscribed by formal delegations of authority emanating, always, from the top. Formal accountability really matters in government, as it should.

Corporate boards, on the other hand, tend to be dominated by two groups: paid managers, and representatives of significant constituencies, notably those that supply the corporation with funds. Formally, of course, the composition of boards of publicly owned corporations is tightly governed by the legal manifestations of the notion of shareholder democracy; privately held corporations tend to be private in order that managers and principal owners, often the same people, can escape the disclosure and representational requirements entailed by public ownership.

In most nonprofits with which I am familiar, the boards are, to all intents and purposes, self-perpetuating, although charters or bylaws may contain certain representational requirements. In most, as well, there are strong mores or formal restrictions enforcing the separation of board from management. I am, for example, the first current or former salaried manager of the United Hospital Fund to serve on its board, and no salaried executive of a member institution ever has.

Historically, of course, the separation of governance from management in nonprofit organizations reflected patterns of status or class. Directors were affluent and socially prominent providers of charity; paid administrators were hired hands. The increasing prevalence of a more "corporate" pattern, in which paid executives sit on boards, may reflect less an increase in their status than a decline in their directors' status!

Every nonprofit board has its own ethics, history, and practices, but several generalizations can be offered based on informal conversations with other managers of nonprofits, along with my own perspective as a member of several such boards. First, the role of chair is clearly quite pivotal, which is remarkable when one remembers that most nonprofit board chairs are part-time, uncompensated volunteers for whom the nonprofit is something quite different from their primary professional or occupational commitment. In many nonprofits, the chair *is* the board, for all practical intents and purposes—other members of the board are controlled by, or defer to, him or her, or really are not terribly interested. More common, I suspect, are the boards where an inner circle of three to six members really exercises control, with the tacit consent of the other members. Some boards, of course, are more seriously fragmented, with multiple factions or cliques which tend to be organized around identifiable personalities or groups rather than fundamentally opposed policy positions.

The relationship between board chair and chief salaried officer is thus the single most important relationship within a nonprofit. When nonprofit managers get together to compare notes, the most positive thing one can say about one's job is how skillful, supportive, and responsible one's board chair is. Far too often, on the other hand, relations between nonprofit boards and managers are perceived as actually or potentially adversarial. Managers may perceive boards as entities to be manipulated, misinformed, or controlled; boards may view managers as dispensable hired hands, who are evaluated more on the basis of degree of deference to the board than on objective performance measures.

If anything, my observation would be that most nonprofit boards (and a smaller proportion of board chairs) are inadequately involved in a systematic way in governance of the organizations. They are not adequately informed; policy-making over which they should have formal jurisdiction is not adequately defined or codified, and board recruitment and development themselves are not paid adequate attention. Effective boards in any organization must function largely through committees; one need only look at the formal committee structure of many nonprofits to realize that they cannot possibly be organized to function effectively (Kovner 1985). I like to think that the United Hospital Fund is an exception to most of these generalizations, but even here, in a relatively large and affluent nonprofit, the issues of board development and adequate staff support for board functions require continuing concern and effort.

Nonprofit managers, whose career backgrounds tend to be in the independent professions or other nonprofits, often resent the degree of authority and informed involvement that boards should exercise as a condition of legitimacy. Conversely, norms of formal authority and legitimacy are inadequately developed in many nonprofit boards. Individual board members may involve themselves inappropriately in seeking to evaluate or even direct staff; decisions of the board may be viewed as binding on staff but not on board members. Policy decisions of considerable magnitude may be reversed or circumvented in relatively cavalier fashion.

In situations of inadequate board performance, or poor executive-board relations, the inherent accountability problems of many nonprofits can pose significant dangers. Without either the formal legitimacy structures of government or the "market test" under which for-profit firms must operate, nonprofits can perform a useful service only to the extent that legitimacy can be derived from a relatively clear expression and implementation of a more or less coherent sense of mission, purpose, or goals. Without such an expression, a central function of any governing board, effective management is impossible almost by definition.

While the legal environment in which nonprofits operate is constructed largely to prevent personal self-aggrandizement by trustees or managers, the more common pathology is irrelevance, as the organization persists in patterns of behavior potentially unrelated to fulfillment of any legitimate purpose. Alternatively, inadequately governed nonprofits are at risk of substituting grant-chasing for goal-setting; whoever offers potential operating funds gets to set the organization's agenda.

In this context, the controversy over the need for, and appropriateness of, "marketing" in nonprofit organizations has some interesting implications. To the extent that marketing consists of a series of activities designed to inform an organization with some sense of mission as to the needs or desires of those it seeks to serve, it can be a kind of preventive medicine to minimize the danger of organizational irrelevancy. To the extent, however, that organizations in which the board fails to articulate a set of goals try to become "market-driven," they have really abandoned all claims to legitimacy.

It is important, of course, not to overgeneralize, nor to mistake pathology for anatomy. Board members of nonprofits are, after all, volunteers, generally (one would hope always) without a direct economic stake in the organization's performance. Their motivations are complex and varied, and complex-varied motivation produces complicated behaviors. But the characteristics of nonprofit governance have particular implications for two especially important aspects of management, in addition to goal-setting and legitimacy: planning and finance.

PLANNING

The degree of faddism associated with various concepts of organizational planning in much of the management literature makes me wary of approaching this subject at all. I have no idea how much systematic strategic or operational planning actually occurs in for-profit corporations, or how much effect such planning activities have on actual behavior. I know from personal experience that government organizations devote a lot of time and effort to planning, with surprisingly little impact on actual behavior. Most nonprofits, as far as I can tell, do hardly any real planning at all. Hospitals in some parts of the country may be something of an exception because of the magnitude of their capital expenditures, which almost demands a planning process, if not real plans, in order to have something to tell the architects and the regulatory authorities. But even in hospitals, planning is generally viewed as a kind of subsidiary function, isolated from top management and board priority-setting processes.

Nonprofits love to conduct "retreats." The board and top management go away together for two or three days to a resort or some other place removed from day-to-day business and spend the time in prolonged discussion of the "big issues." The more sophisticated the nonprofit, the more money it will invest in preparing for the retreat by developing handsome briefing books, hiring consultants and facilitators, and so forth.

Such retreats, in my experience, actually perform two important functions. First, and not to be minimized, they provide an opportunity for substantially improved social interaction among board members, and between board and staff, which tends to carry over, at least for a while, into improved relationships and nicer organizational tone. Second, and more important, well-run retreats produce discussion about goals, and often substantial progress in developing consensus about the goals of the organization.

Development of such goal consensus is, of course, most difficult in nonprofits, which lack both the for-profits' bottom-line tests and public agencies' electoral tests. Some degree of clarity about goals is essential for organizational effectiveness. But goal-setting is only the *first step* in planning. Unfortunately, it seems to be as far as most nonprofits get.

I would hypothesize that the very process of developing, maintaining, and protecting goal consensus consumes so much organizational energy and so much managerial time and attention, in most nonprofits, that there is not enough left over for very much real planning (Perrow 1961). In particular, I think nonprofits are probably excessively risk-averse, because effective strategic risk-taking involves real strategic planning of a sort in which few nonprofits engage. Certainly, the sorts of redeployment of assets, entry and withdrawal from various lines of business, and continual exploration of both merger and divestment activities that characterize the corporate sector tend to occur among nonprofits only in response to crises or to vigorous external pushing or prodding from governments or other organizations.

Perhaps—another hypothesis—one reason nonprofits have proliferated numerically to such an extent is that the birth rate so exceeds the death rate, and new problems or "markets" tend to be filled by new nonprofits rather than by strategic entry from older ones (Young 1983, p. 9).

FINANCE

Of course, nonprofits may be risk-averse because of problems in their capital structure. The literature on nonprofits and their economies devotes considerable attention to the problem of performance tests in the absence of a profit criterion, and to the dependence of nonprofits on particularly undependable revenue sources, such as governments. But not enough attention has been paid, I suspect, to the capital structure of nonprofits and the implications of those capital structures for management.

The most basic general observation about the capital structure of nonprofits is that there is not very much. The second, closely related, observation is that it is hard to get more. Hospitals, foundations, and universities are the major exceptions, but most hospitals have something in excess of their total capitalization tied up in physical plant and equipment; foundations are hardly anything *but* big piles of capital; and I do not claim to be able even to begin to understand universities. The fact is that, for most other nonprofits, capital is scarce, inadequate, and hard to obtain.

Nonprofits, of course, cannot issue stock, or at least stock that anyone would want to buy; they cannot borrow very much, except for buildings that will generate revenue, since lenders are not entirely stupid; and traditionally they have not been able to amass very much through retained earnings, since the ethos of nonprofits frowned heavily on retained earnings in the rare instances when they were attainable to begin with. Furthermore, one of the most powerful generators of capital, the Internal Revenue Code, has been essentially unavailable by definition to nonprofits. Accelerated depreciation, loss carry forwards, leveraged leases, and—except for one brief moment in time—even sheltered sale-leasebacks have availed nonprofits hardly at all.

Nonprofits have essentially only two ways of generating capital. Someone can give it to them. Or they can wisely invest assets someone gave them in the past. Occasionally, they can generate surpluses by selling services for more than cost, but such opportunities tend to be short-lived, since if market conditions that permit such surpluses persist, for-profit firms are likely to enter and cream off the most profitable opportunities.

The chronic capital shortages of most nonprofits have a number of managerial implications. At the most elementary level, nonprofit managers spend a disproportionate share of their time worrying about real estate since, unless someone has given them a building, they are not only renters but, from landlords' perspectives, not particularly desirable tenants. Their finances are often perilous; they generate lots of human traffic, sometimes including social "undesirables," and remain open all sorts of odd hours.

Nonprofit managers must also, of course, devote a lot of time and energy to raising money. There is nothing inherently wrong with that, except that the professional training and background of most nonprofit managers not only fail to equip them for fundraising, but also tend to attach negative connotations to such activity. Fundraising is perceived by a large proportion of nonprofit managers as inherently distasteful, outside the scope of their professional orientation, and a diversion from their primary tasks. It is surprising, given such attitudes, how good at it so many of them get to be.

Most important, chronic capital shortages make program innovation difficult. Organizations that budget to break even at existing operational levels, have little by way of reserves, and have difficulty obtaining access to venture capital cannot innovate as well as they should. Since the rate of return calculus does not really apply to them either, even the prospect of great "rewards" creates little incentive. The risks from failure are disproportionate to the possible benefits of success. Failure can mean financial difficulty, or public embarrassment, or a truncated career. Success only engenders more work.

HUMAN RESOURCES

What nonprofits lack in financial capital they have often made up for in people. The nonprofit sector functions as well as it does, indeed functions at all, because of its ability to tap the energies and skills of employees and volunteers at an economic cost much lower than other sectors have to face.

The relationship between nonprofit organizations and their employees has three critical dimensions. First, the economic logic of much of the nonprofit sector has historically been based on underpayment of its employees. In the starkest but by no means trivial case, priests, nuns, and other religious, paid literally at subsistence levels, long provided the economic backbone of parochial schools, many religious hospitals, and other institutions. Nonprofits were for many years exempted from federal labor laws and even Social Security. In the last two decades, the payment gap between nonprofits and other employers has shrunk considerably, but the difference persists to a perhaps alarming degree.

Customarily, the underpayment of nonprofit employees was ostensibly counterbalanced by lower performance expectations and high levels of job security. The managerial implications of those mores are obvious and frustrating. It is one thing to attempt, in difficult economic times, to redress longstanding inequities in compensation, but managers are damned if they do and damned if they don't in efforts to accompany compensation adjustments with parallel changes in expectations for employee performance.

The difficulty in raising performance expectations is not unrelated to the second critical dimension of nonprofit employment, the concentration of employees in a relatively small number of professional and occupational categories that have traditionally been predominantly female and underpaid. Nurses, social workers, teachers, and secretaries, for example, often share professional or peer group norms that may or may not be congruent with a manager's particular agenda—and the managers are disproportionately likely to be male, although the disproportion in the nonprofit sector, to that sector's great credit, is significantly less than in the for-profit sector (Butter et al. 1987). Nonprofit managers either devote considerable time and energy to negotiating (explicitly or, more important, implicitly) with their employees over the terms and conditions of employment, or else pay a price in terms of organizational performance.

Professional and organizational subcultures also have so much force in many nonprofits, I suspect, because formal personnel administration tends to be so inadequate. Nonprofits are not very good at personnel administration, in large part, because historically they did not have to be; they could get and keep cheap female labor when they needed it. Nonprofits, of course, also tend to be small, which can be a problem itself in terms of the mechanics of personnel administration. But in a world of *ERISA* (Employee Retirement Income Security Act), Title VII, and higher employee expectations, nonprofits are being held to higher standards. Meeting those standards is a major challenge for nonprofit managers.

Finally, values (goals, ideology, mission) are important in all aspects of nonprofit administration, but nowhere more so than in the management of human resources. The values of the nonprofit organization are, of course, a primary source of motivation for its staff, and a partial explanation for the organization's ability to attract and retain talented people.

The importance of the organization's values to its people has a twofold implication for managers. First, effective communication to all staff about organizational purposes, ends and means, and basic value commitments is a central and continual managerial function. Second, management must insure some degree of consistency between the organization's stated objectives and the way it behaves toward its own employees and other constituents. A nonprofit can, in theory, be good at meeting principal objectives and be a lousy employer at the same time, but doing so resembles trying to drive from one place to another entirely in reverse.

Congruence between a nonprofit's programmatic goals and how it behaves toward people is an especially difficult issue when those people are volunteers associated with the organization. Many nonprofits remain critically dependent on volunteers for fundraising, community relations, and direct service provision, but most act as though they would rather they did not. Overworked and underpaid professional staff, generally with little or no formal training in working with volunteers, require not only supervision but constant reinforcement as to the meaning and worth of volunteer activity. Volunteer recruitment, development, training, and noneconomic "compensation" must be addressed just as the same issues are addressed for paid staff. And the role of volunteers in the organization must be incorporated into the planning and budgeting process rather than being treated as a gratuitous afterthought. What, after all, is a voluntary organization without volunteers?

LEADERSHIP

The articulation and communication of organizational goals and mission are, of course, a fundamental attribute of leadership, but they are just one of the dimensions along which successful management of nonprofits requires successful leadership by managers. "The system" will not suffice. Generally, there is no system to fall back on. Both because of their size and, perhaps ironically, because they are protected from various reporting and disclosure requirements in the tax and securities laws, many nonprofits may be insufficiently bureaucratized for their own good.

The problems of goal consensus, of constraints on formal planning, of limited access to capital, of maintaining motivation and morale among both employees and volunteers, all demand a quality of personal leadership if the organization is to succeed and thrive. The exact forms such leadership will take hinge critically, of course, on particular organizational and environmental circumstances and on the history and orientation of the organization. I do not think there is any real substitute.

Even assuming, for purposes of discussion, an adequate supply of leadership skills among nonprofit managers, dependence on these skills creates serious, if unavoidable, problems. In the Weberian terminology I learned in graduate school, the institutionalization of charisma is a task that many nonprofits can never successfully accomplish; they are too small, or too dependent on a shifting environment, or too dominated by professional ideologies, or too uncertain of their own goals. The history of many nonprofits, to a much greater extent than corporations or government agencies, is a series of biographies—of board leaders and senior managers. Too many thriving nonprofits fall on hard times during leadership interregnums; too many others lurch from one leadership style to another. The most important task for any manager is to arrange a suitable and timely succession. In Weberian terms, again, charismatic leaders are the least able to institutionalize their own roles (Weber 1947). But that is the single most important thing nonprofit managers have to do better and must be taught to do better.

The central importance of leadership is far greater for nonprofits than for either business or government agencies; it also poses difficult challenges for those seeking to educate nonprofit managers. No itemized lists of skills or "competencies" will suffice, although written and oral communication are indispensable. The very dissimilar British and Chinese empires thrived under leaders educated in their very dissimilar classics, and atrophied under similarly trained leaders. Nonetheless, sensitivity as well as strong commitment to value issues is obviously indispensable, as is the capacity to articulate them.

CONCLUSIONS

Any analysis of problems encountered by managers runs the risk, of course, of painting a unilaterally and unrealistically dreary picture. For good reasons, in fact, most nonprofits, when they look for managers, have no shortage of applicants (though how qualified those applicants might be is another question). There are obviously some very real rewards.

For one thing, nonprofits have the virtues of their defects. Problems of governance require paying lots of attention both to personal relationships with highly motivated and often very interesting people. Difficulties in institutional planning require managers to develop their own visions, be able to interpret those visions in changing circumstances, and move them to fruition. Capital shortages put a premium on creativity, ingenuity, and cleverness. Effective management of human resources requires us would-be social reformers to put our actions where we think our principles are. And the demand for effective leadership is the greatest challenge of all.

The very dependence of nonprofits on successful leadership, while generating serious risks of excessive ego inflation and fatuous self-importance, also means that nonprofit management can provide an opportunity, of a sort increasingly rare in modern society, to match one's personal values and beliefs with the requirements of one's job. The gap between one's ultimate and instrumental goals can be narrower in nonprofit management than in almost any other job one can imagine. Many nonprofit managers' occupational activities are of course directly a result of religious or moral convictions; their occupations are quite literally their vocations. For secular humanists, on the other hand, nonprofit work is the closest they can come to doing God's work.

6

Different Types of Nonprofit Managers

Simon Slavin

The organizational and managerial literature deals extensively with hierarchies and bureaucratic structure as well as with related problems associated with authority, control, responsibility, and the like. At first glance, however, the examination of hierarchies does not seem to be a promising subject for generating insight into the graduate training of managerial personnel in nonprofit organizations. Yet, the differences between nonprofit management and management of other types of organizations with respect to the nature of specific management levels and positions are neither trivial nor without relevance to the central concerns of this book. I will suggest that the differences are pregnant with meaning for educational strategies and training protocols.

Much of what follows is drawn from the central distinction between profit and nonprofit organizations. The former are businesses operating in the marketplace; this inevitably dictates their preoccupations and strategies. They are subject to the potentialities and constraints of the economic institutions that circumscribe them. Their field of vision goes far beyond the operation organized to produce their products. Thus, they are subject to the vagaries affecting financing, tax considerations, relationship to investments, and other externalities not essentially related to the organization of internal resources for meeting consumer demands. The essential unifying interest is return on investment, which in turn affects all other stated and implied purposes. Their criterion for organizational success is generally clear and unambiguous, particularly in the long run, and can be discerned by a glance at the balance sheet.

In his discussion of the performance of the service institutions and the business enterprise, Drucker (1973, p. 45) states:

Service is in a fundamentally different "business" from business. It is different in its purpose. It has different values. It needs different objectives. And it makes a different contribution to society. "Performance and results" are quite different in a service institution from what they are in a business. "Managing for performance" is the one area in which the service institution differs significantly from a business.

It is in the performance of the respective institutions that there are telling lessons for the issues we are exploring.

The nonprofit organization functions essentially in the service system where the evaluation and judgments of organizational effectiveness are based on the effects and consequence of the actual encounter with service recipients. Here criteria are less clear-cut, often vague, intangible, and generally nonquantitative. Organizational members are largely composed of professionals trained in specialized fields centrally related to their organization's sphere of operation.

Widely diversified professional cultures abound in the nonprofit sector. Distinctive histories, established traditions, and specialized training protocols characterize the major subgroups. These dissimilarities have a significant impact on the way these organizations deal with managerial hierarchies. Because of the wide array of nonprofit enterprises, few generalizations hold with respect to particular aspects of their work, although there surely are, at higher levels of abstraction, many common characteristics. In comparison with profit-making organizations, substantial differences affect the relationship between higher and lower organizational levels.

One way in which to examine these internal dynamics is to look at two modes in which organizations pursue the achievement of their objectives. On the one hand, there are the behaviors of organizational functionaries who deliver particular products designed by the delivery system. They deal with the skills and knowledge necessary to achieve organizational purposes. On the other hand, there are various behaviors that facilitate and enhance the organization's capacity to perform its implied and explicit functions. The latter deals with instrumental actions, the former with the achievement of substantive targets. Akin to the polarities between means and ends, this distinction counterposes efficiency variables to effectiveness variables.

Instrumental functions are widely generalized in organizations. They serve largely common needs of both profit and nonprofit pursuits. They deal with such matters as information handling, accounting systems, interpretation and computer technology, fund gathering, and financial management. Although these functions bend in some ways to the specific needs of diverse organizations, they constitute commonly applied processes.

Alternatively, expressive or substantive functions tend to be highly individual, varying from enterprise to enterprise, discrete in the use of specialized technologies, philosophies, tools, and approaches. This distinction has potent meaning for levels of work since they tend to affect profit and nonprofit hierarchies differently. The very diversity of nonprofit enterprises, in substance, size, complexity, and objectives, provides testimony to the uniqueness of classes of nonprofits.

Neighborhood associations and ballet companies, country clubs and hospitals, are sharply delineated by professional requirements. Focusing on these distinctive characteristics need not dilute their common needs for supporting managerial practices. To the contrary, relating and adapting such practices to the requirements of competent service delivery provide their essential organizational task—meeting the human and social needs to which the nonprofit organization owes its genesis. An encompassing view of the nonprofit endeavor envisions purpose and substance as one side of the organizational equation, the other side balanced by instrumental managerial operations that make their achievement possible. Each side is essential and necessary but in itself insufficient for organizational fulfillment.

The distance between higher and lower incumbents with respect to instrumental functions is considerably narrower than that between corresponding expressive functions. I mean by this that the kinds of knowledge and skill are less differentiated in the former than in the latter. Moving up the ladder in position and authority largely requires the use of similar conceptual categories of work, even though the actual behaviors call for an expanded conception of the uses of authority and control. The essential concern for profit maximization, return on investment, or share of market calls for a hierarchy of rule-making that varies little from business to business. Rule-making and rule-conforming behavior at each organizational level are guided by common canons of efficiency that yield distributional surplus.

Since I want to make the case that the profit system of organization relies more heavily on instrumental than expressive functions ("behavior in large for-profit or bureaucratic organizations is evaluated in instrumental terms"—Majone 1980, p. 23), it may be instructive to examine the way in which schools of business administration organize their curricula. In one leading graduate program of studies, for instance, more than one hundred courses are listed, only two or three of which might be thought to deal with specialized product content. All deal with business operations as a unitary whole, essentially involving instrumental technology—accounting, business economics and public policy, finance, information systems, organizational management, research, and marketing. Presumably, these offerings provide a sufficient and necessary preparation for entering business and industry. Significantly, business school graduates evince little intrinsic interest in a particular kind of business, preferring to choose opportunities that promise greater income and career advancement per se.

Career paths in business frequently move from one kind of activity to another. This is generally possible because superordinate and subordinate relationships are concerned with generally similar conceptual problems and issues in spite of differences in particular arenas of business activity.

The argument is sometimes made that business management suffers from this emphasis on training in common processes, and that business education should focus more on distinctive content in such matters as technology and production processes. It may be the case that high technology businesses which depend on advanced, sophisticated technical competence present additional requirements for management. In this respect they somewhat resemble profession-based nonprofit organizations. However, for the more general run of market-based organizations, focused as they are on essentially similar ultimate objectives and central processes, the continued and increased demands in recent decades for business school graduates to staff management positions in business enterprises suggest satisfaction with the products of existing generic education.

By way of contrast, in the nonprofit social services the graduate curriculum in social work in the same university noted above offers eighty-one courses, of which thirty-seven deal with specific content areas. Such programs have always been concerned with this generic-specific dilemma. Currently, most social work schools organize at least half of their curricula around specialized fields of practice. In varying degrees, the same appears to be true in the other major fields of nonprofit activity—health, education, and the arts.

It might be thought that this is an unfair comparison since business schools train managers while schools of social work primarily prepare service providers. But this is a too limited view of the educational product of the latter, which has increasingly designed curricula that train nonclinical practitioners such as administrators, social planners, and social policy analysts. In each instance, knowledge and skill are based on the generic professional ingredients rooted in the values, ethics, and philosophy guiding service delivery of the social agency system. The fact that service-providing technology coexists in a symbiotic relationship with service-facilitating technology suggests the holistic character of profession-based organizational systems.

The contrast implicit in the technical-instrumental and substantive-expressive dichotomy is perhaps best seen in organizations dealing with the creative arts. They frequently recognize these respective orientations in the formal structure of their organizations. Some have separated these functions at the highest level of authority and have in effect established two parallel hierarchies.

The experience of the Metropolitan Opera provides a recent illustration. After many decades during which a single executive was responsible for the total direction of that organization, the company divided its executive leadership, establishing the positions of general manager and artistic director. The general manager is responsible for such activities as fundraising, union negotiations, the care and upkeep of the house, work with public and federal agencies, and maintaining relations with significant constituencies. Artistic control and musical policy rest with the artistic director. This dual executive leadership reflects a recognition of the variant demands made by technical-supportive operations in contrast to the substantive nature of the artistic enterprise. As general manager, the former head of a major public relations firm was selected even though lacking prior experience in arts management. Somewhat similar arrangements have been made in the management of the Metropolitan Museum of Art in New York. The Houston Ballet Company created a "troika" of executives comprised of a director of administration and marketing, an artistic director, and a director of planning and development.

That business executives can move easily into the technical managerial area in nonprofit organizations in fields far removed from their profit-oriented experience suggests that business experience tends to be generic. Transferability of roles is possible because the skills necessary for occupying upper-level positions are only modestly differentiated. As people move from one level to another, their preoccupations become broader, but the problems they confront have a similar direction. That is why it is appropriate to train business personnel in a unified curriculum that deals, both conceptually and practically, with matters applying across the board to market-based enterprises.

These organizational arrangements in the museum, opera, and ballet companies may be deviant and reflect the effect of organizational size and complexity as well as special temporal circumstances. More typical is the experience of both the American Ballet Theatre and the New York City Ballet, where distinguished artists serve as overall directors, presumably engaging technical personnel to deal with nonartistic support activities. In a recent interview, Peter Martins, director of the New York City Ballet, was quoted as saying (*New York Times,* May 4, 1986, p. 21), "I can't conceive of being the head of a ballet company without having been a ballet dancer. Or a dancer in any form." Implicit in this comment is the integral conception of executive leadership in highly differentiated enterprises in which extended professional study and training are required for effective organizational performance. Such specialized training is in addition, of course, to training in dealing with more universal organizational dynamics.

The demands placed on management by both sets of functions in nonprofit activities make the task of supervising successive levels of management personnel more complex and severe than in the business realm. The more esoteric the knowledge and skill requirements for personnel in the delivery system, the more evident this degree of severity becomes. This may explain why there is so much conflict and contention in organizations concerned with the creative arts. In the aesthetic realm are to be found people who are socialized through distinctive cultures, seemingly removed from the pragmatic demands of day-to-day reality testing.

The place of the professions in nonprofit organizations has special significance for issues concerning the management of hierarchies. In the fields of social welfare, education, and health, the professions of social work, teaching, and medicine provide the personnel structure necessary for effective service delivery. Upward mobility begins at the service level; career advancement is based on the recognition of competent professional performance. In each case, professionals supervise and manage other professionals with similar training and experience. When organizations in these fields employ managers from distant or disparate fields, strain tends to develop.

Two illustrations in the field of social welfare come to mind. In a large eastern city a major planning and funding agency retired two co-executives of very long tenure. They expanded their search and selected a superintendent of schools from a nearby community who had developed a substantial reputation for managerial and educational leadership. The new incumbent lasted barely one year, after which a noted social worker was engaged.

In the same city, a large and venerable social agency selected as its new executive a person noted for his leadership in religious organizations. The consequences of this choice were disastrous; after one year a replacement from within the profession was hired.

Professionals do not take well to control by nonprofessionals or professionals from fields removed from their own. After numerous studies, the Brunel group in England concluded that "at a certain stage of development the possibility of managerial control of professional members by non-members must be excluded. This happens when the latter can no longer judge the competence of such professionals nor assess the technical problems encountered" (Jaques 1978, p. 329).

In the foregoing nonprofit organizations there are, in effect, dual sets of skill and knowledge required for managerial competence—the technical and the substantive. One deals with managerial science and related organizational theories and concepts. The other relies on respective professional theories and concepts, and related social and behavioral science. Where there is a central emphasis on professional practice, the differences between managerial levels in profit and nonprofit enterprises are substantial. However, not all nonprofit organizations engage personnel from the professions or from areas that require extended theoretical study and practical experience. To the extent that this is true the differences between these two systems are minimal.

These issues come into sharpest focus when fields that have traditionally been voluntary and not-for-profit begin to develop forays into the marketplace. In social welfare there are four areas in recent years in which this has been especially noted—nursing home care, day care, child welfare, and health care. In the health area, 1,100 general hospitals belonged to investor-owned hospital chains in 1984 (Gilbert 1985, p. 369). This shift in central objectives from service to profit is also a move toward incorporating a dominant instrumental orientation. As many have noted, the profit constraint can distort organizational goals and action, resulting in goal substitution and displacement (DiMaggio 1983, p. 29; Kramer 1985a, p. 388; Riechert 1977). In one dramatic incident recently reported (*New York Times,* May 4, 1986), a for-profit hospital promised doctors cash bonuses, free meals, and free rounds of golf for bringing in patients. In a letter to staff physicians, the administrator and part-owner of the hospital wrote, "Any doctor that has 10 or more inpatient admissions in one month will have the choice of dinner for two or one round of golf at the Country Club" (p. 44). Here is a graphic example of the substitution of profit for service goals, undoubtedly an extreme instance.

Instrumental ends tend to be quantifiable and measurable and are often pursued at the expense of substantive goals. "Agencies under great pressure to measure what they do . . . tend to do only those things they can measure. . . . The drive to efficiency can thus lead to undervaluation of the qualitative, often hard-to-measure components of social services" (Gilbert 1985, p. 375). Pressures of the marketplace often tend to place the integrity of the service at risk.

Implicit in the question under discussion is the issue of transferability of managerial skills. If the differences in managing hierarchies in profit and nonprofit endeavors are insignificant, people trained as managers in the abstract, divorced from the specifics of organizational purpose, should be able to provide leadership in any and all types of organizations. I have tried to suggest that these differences are indeed marked in broad segments of nonprofit organizations. The existence of a universal "managerial man," like that of "economic man," is largely mythic. The tasks confronting managers are too diverse in the wide array of settings in which they work. This is particularly true in the specialized agencies motivated by other goals than financial return on investment.

It is sometimes suggested that there are two contrasting types of administrative personality—the professional (program) versus the managerial (business). I would suggest that this states a false dichotomy. The competent executive in a modern-day nonprofit organization, regardless of his or her specific position, must be properly equipped in both the professional and the business dimensions. There is a general consensus that the essential function of the administrator is to chart and monitor the life of some part of the organization. At minimum this involves setting direction (policy), establishing goals and objectives, developing strategies to achieve them, and pursuing the technical means that enhance these pursuits. All this requires a fusion of knowledge and skills of both instrumental and expressive dimensions suggesting the importance of conceptualizing a particularistic rather than a universal administration.

Another perspective for viewing such issues is through an understanding of the nature of organizational culture. Schein (1985, p. 9) defines culture as a pattern of basic assumptions and beliefs. These develop out of shared learning, common and validated experiences, and, above all, consensual values. Taken together these attributes define an occupational community or profession. Those who come from the same host culture function within a common value framework and pursue common endeavors. Culture also includes norms, roles, status, and sentiments. Each plays its part in fashioning behavior expectations and in establishing patterns of individual and group behavior. Those who perform professional functions assume status positions beyond those of organizational technicians. Doctors in hospitals outrank those who carry administrative responsibilities, as do professionals in education, social welfare, and religion.

The potentiality for organizational conflict and goal distortion is exacerbated when people socialized in divergent cultures meet under the same umbrella. Because nonprofit organizations need to employ personnel with varying cultural conditioning—some dealing with purely organizational dimensions and others from specific cultural realms—the problems faced by managers tend to be relatively severe. Management in the business profit culture deals with many problems and issues, but cultural diversity tends not to add substantially to these burdens.

This brief examination of hierarchical relationships in profit and nonprofit organizations has some meaning for the central preoccupation of this book—the advanced training of nonprofit managerial personnel. Having pointed to some significant differences between these two classes of organizations, as well as some differences that surface when the array of nonprofits is disaggregated, some conclusions seem indicated. The MBA model for training managers in market-based organizations is not really transferable to those functioning outside the market. The structural and substantive differences between the two types of organizations are simply too great. The organizing principles and central purposes are too disparate, and these tend to shape their essential activities.

However, since nonprofit organizations employ managers of generic functions such as accounting, finance, and information systems, can generic training prepare them for successful operation in the nonprofit setting? If so, should one then posit two kinds of nonprofit managers—business (generic) and program (substantive)? While two kinds of knowledge and skill are implicit in this distinction, effective top management, as suggested above, combines both qualities in productive interaction. Administrators who are responsible for charting and monitoring an organization's destiny are constantly involved in decision-making affecting the ways in which it responds to the demands of the internal and external environments in the light of overriding mission and objectives. Such decisions invariably require knowing intimately the nature of the enterprise, knowledge born of thoroughgoing training and experience.

Program personnel who have come through professional education move, in time, into managerial positions. What they require for competency is further development of the technical ("business side") requisites for true managerial leadership. When this is achieved such managers combine both program *and* generic business attributes, the latter serving the purposes of the former. General organizational management or executive roles are then well served.

Is the reverse relationship between business and program skill as cogent? Can business personnel effectively assume executive responsibilities for non-profit ventures? The answer is "yes" only in profession-dominated enterprises if they go through the rigors of professional socialization and training, adding insight thus gained to their managerial skill repertoire. Without such preparation, decisions respecting professional issues and options will inevitably be circumscribed.

There are, thus, two kinds of managers—those who manage programs and those who manage business operations, as long as these are delineated scopes of activity. And both are necessary for nonprofit effectiveness. But for general organizational management, encompassing the more total life space of the organization, there is optimally one kind of manager, one who is equipped at varying points in the hierarchy to supervise, monitor, and direct operations in their totality.

A singular model for the training of all nonprofit managerial personnel paralleling the cognate patterns developed by schools of business is not adequate to this task. It is difficult to see how the same comprehensive curriculum can encompass the requirements necessary to achieve the specialized purposes of museums, religious organizations, and child welfare agencies. At some level of abstraction there are structures and processes that have common import for varying nonprofit enterprises. Such matters as board functions and structures, philanthropy and fundraising, grants and subsidies, relations with governmental agencies, accounting protocols, and adapting information systems interest all nonprofits in ways that distinguish them from their profit-oriented relatives.

There is thus a distinctive core of knowledge and skill behavior that permeates nonprofit enterprises. Together with principles and practices derived from the literature on organizational theory and dynamics, they constitute an essential basis for educating managerial personnel in this field of work. For nonprofit organizations which do not base their work on particular professions, such a curriculum might also be sufficient for competent administration. However, in the major nonprofit fields of education, health, religion, the arts, and social welfare, which together account for 80 percent of total employment in this sector (Program on Nonprofit Organizations, 1984, p. 2), much more than this basic core is required for performance competence. Without the incorporation of distinctive professional cultures and values into the educational process, managerial personnel can hardly be prepared to provide that broad-visioned administrative direction which alone can achieve relevant and significant organizational goals. Managerial leadership at its best combines sensitivity, skill, and knowledge of both technical means and substantive purposes. One path to take along this route is to develop cooperative, coordinated programs with the relevant professional schools in the university setting. Ample precedent exists for such combined effort in a variety of fields. Coordinated protocols can avoid competitive struggle over turf and claims of ascendency.

Schools of social work have for some years developed cooperative programs with law schools within the same university. Students were able to achieve joint degrees, focusing on legal problems affecting social welfare clients in such areas as child welfare, child custody, marital and separation difficulties, and mental health (commitment to psychiatric institutions). A number of universities have ongoing programs leading to joint degrees in social work and business administration. They also accept relevant offerings for respective graduate credits in their individual degrees. Columbia University School of Social Work has recently established cooperative offerings with two seminaries, granting faculty status to selected members of their respective faculties.

The time is clearly ripe for a greater focus on the place of the nonprofit enterprise in a nation that is increasingly oriented to a service economy. What is especially indicated is an intensification of research, particularly comparative administrative research. In-depth study of profit and nonprofit programs and practices revealing both differences and commonalities will surely add to the professional equipment of both areas. Similarly, comparative study within the nonprofit fraternity should enhance an understanding of both generics and specifics. A promising line of inquiry in this direction would be the study of levels of managerial responsibilities in both forms of organizational enterprises. Fortunately, there exists an important, though neglected, body of work stemming out of the research of Elliott Jaques and his collaborators at the Brunel Institute of Organization and Social Studies in England.

For many years Jaques has been concerned with the natural division of managerial responsibility in organizations. Beginning with his study of the Glacier Project (Jaques 1965), his findings were elaborated in his *General Theory of Bureaucracy* (Jaques 1976). He found that manager–subordinate role relations have observable boundaries that constitute real strata in a universally applicable depth-structure. These conclusions, he claims, have been validated in studies in a number of countries and in a multiplicity of organizations. According to Jaques, there are five clearly articulated levels of organization and managerial capacity "that are not expressed in quantitative continuous increases or decreases of information, skill or ability, but in qualitatively different ways of organizing action and experiences into structured wholes" (Stamp 1978, p. 251, pp. 258–259; Rowbottom and Billis 1978, pp. 118ff.; and Billis 1984 delineate related schemes).

In a similar vein, Patti (1983, p. 45) has distinguished four levels of work in social welfare organizations, as follows:

1. Program staff level; concern is with the direct contact with consumer–clients, the point at which the organization's service is delivered;

2. Supervisory management level; primarily involved in developing and facilitating technical and professional processes;

3. Program management level; sometimes referred to as mid–level management, responsible for devising the means the organization uses to accomplish its goals and objectives;

4. Executive management level; provides overall leadership and direction for the enterprise, formulates policy and maintains essential relationships with related external groups and organizations.

Each of these levels performs distinctive functions requiring different skills on the part of managerial incumbents. Their placement in the organizational hierarchy establishes the ways in which authority and control are allocated and contributes to their central charge, that of maintaining the integrity and survival of the organization. "The manager in each level is accountable for his subordinates' work in all its aspects; . . . is able to assess the quality and effectiveness of his subordinates' work as it is done, and . . . has the authority to make further prescriptions or reassignments of work which he may judge to be necessary" (Rowbottom 1978, p. 75).

An examination of the characteristics of various managerial levels suggests that they move from the concrete and specific to the more generic, more abstract, and more broadly encompassed. Each level is increasingly removed from the point in the delivery system where the consumer transaction takes place, and tends to focus on problems and issues that affect the organization's internal and external constituencies. Increasingly, contributions are made to the planning and coordination of the organization's activities. At each level there are broader realms of discretion and decision-making, and the consequences of managerial judgment become more severe for organizational strength and survival.

The manager's work orientation, wherever it is placed, derives from the objectives that the organization strives to achieve. The fulfillment of these objectives, which begins at the lowest level of the organization, radiates throughout each of the subsequent levels. The special relationships of stratum managers to the achievement of central objectives should cast some light on the differences between profit and nonprofit enterprises with respect to the relationship between the strata. Such a comparative view should provide some perspectives on our central inquiry: are these differences greater for one than for the other? I have tried to suggest that they are indeed greater for much of the field, and that these differences bear significant meaning for advanced education of nonprofit managers.

7

The Development of Useful Curricula for Nonprofit Management

Robert F. Leduc and Terry W. McAdam

This chapter discusses a number of the key issues that must be addressed in the development of useful curricula for nonprofit management. It is based on more than a decade of our own experience developing and teaching courses and mini-courses on subjects related to nonprofit management.

There is a real need for increased attention to the education and development of nonprofit managers. As Brian O'Connell, the president of Independent Sector, recently stated: "Our sector is the only one of the three sectors that does not yet invest heavily in the development of future leadership. We are so scattered and so preoccupied with immediate human needs and aspirations that almost no one has the time, money, and responsibility to attend to the fundamentals of future effectiveness" (McAdam 1986, p. xii). This sector needs to invest more heavily in its human resources. Advanced training through a high-quality curriculum on nonprofit management is one promising approach.

This chapter contains a discussion of seven issues that affect the content and character of curricula for nonprofit management. They are discussed below in no particular order. Different readers will find some issues more relevant to their particular situation than others.

What should be the appropriate mix between generic and specific management education?

This issue can be conceptualized in three different ways:

- *Field-specific education,* such as education regarding the management of health care delivery, the arts, educational institutions, religious organizations, human service programs, and professional and trade associations.

It should be noted that several of the subfields of the independent sector are already being addressed within the university. Hospital administration is presently being taught within graduate schools of business, graduate schools of public affairs, medical schools, and schools of public health in many universities across the country. Graduate schools of education teach management to future leaders of schools and academic institutions; graduate schools of social work offer a specific track in administration, primarily for human service organizations; and there are several programs in arts administration around the country.

- *Basic or generic management education* in fields such as human resources management, marketing, finance, accounting, economics, organization theory, or any of the other subtopics of nonprofit management.

    While it is true that basic models of management may be transferable to the nonprofit sector, it is also true that general management principles alone are not sufficient for management education in the nonprofit sector. Generic management principles and models must be taught in conjunction with the culture of the nonprofit sector. Nonprofit managers are required to apply a set of values that reflect the context of a sector steeped in a rich volunteer tradition. These values must be preserved and integrated into a generic management curriculum.

- *Applied or specific nonprofit sector management education* treating topics such as fund accounting as a special application of basic accounting, volunteer management as a component of human resources management important to the nonprofit sector, and fundraising as an important aspect of financial resource development.

    Unlike the government and business sectors, the nonprofit sector relies on charitable donations and a largely volunteer staffing and governance system. Therefore, nonprofit management education must focus its curriculum on the aspects that undergird this sector. For example, teaching the principles of fundraising as an application of resource development—how to raise funds, write proposals, appeal to foundations and corporations—is an essential component of this form of professional education.

The optimal nonprofit sector management curriculum will contain a blend of all three of these perspectives.

What is the appropriate instructional setting for a nonprofit management course of study?

There is no correct answer here. The most important factor will be to identify or create a setting that will be hospitable and supportive for both students and faculty. Viable programs seem to operate now in graduate schools of business administration, public administration, social work, and several other disciplines. In addition, there are joint programs that operate in partnerships among schools of fine arts, public health, and urban affairs, to name just a few. However, research by one of us in 1984 found that eighty-three "experts" in the field of nonprofit organization management were overwhelmingly of the opinion that the best sites for such training were schools of business administration or schools of public administration.

How should the curriculum be structured?

Curriculum is the substance of professional education and the basis for establishing a set of learning experiences for the student interested in non-profit management. A nonprofit curriculum should assemble courses and experiences to develop the student's capacity to think critically, to analyze situations, to synthesize data, and to relate theories to practice.

Rather than list an entire curriculum here, we would like to advance a series of topics that should be treated in an effective nonprofit management curriculum. We believe that courses offered to nonprofit organization managers should be provided in conjunction with the core courses in a graduate school of administration; the latter may include some or all of the following:

- Economics
- Finance and budgeting
- Accounting
- Organizational theory and behavior
- Statistics
- Human resources management
- Management information systems

The nonprofit-management-specific topics that should be available to the student include the following:

- The history of philanthropy and the nonprofit sector
- The philosophical, ethical, and value issues involved in the sector
- Marketing/public relations/advertising/promotion
- Governance
- Policy formation
- Resource development (fundraising, volunteer management, securing nonfinancial and in-kind resources, etc.)
- Entrepreneurship
- Management control and evaluation
- Strategic and program planning
- Law and taxes
- Advocacy (lobbying, public education, and community leadership)

Who should teach the nonprofit management curriculum?

Given the diversity of the nonprofit sector and those who work in it, it makes sense to draw upon a variety of disciplines for instruction. In most universities and colleges there may be faculty within different schools and departments who can and will want to contribute to a good nonprofit management program. Local practitioners can also offer considerable depth in terms of concrete skills and practical experience which will be useful to the student.

There are several considerations, pro and con, relative to the use of adjunct professors:

- Adjunct faculty hold down labor costs, but this is sometimes viewed as exploitation due to the large disparity in payment per course taught by full-time versus part-time faculty.
- Adjunct faculty ensure a more diverse teaching force with stronger representation from people in direct practitioner roles.
- Adjunct instructors can be critical to assembling an adequate faculty if larger programs are to be mounted.
- Adjunct faculty represent the broader community.

It may be argued that adjunct professors will have very limited value for doctoral students, since the adjuncts may lack the research and theory-building experience necessary to this level of education. At the master's level, however, we believe that adjuncts can relate very well to mid-career students, who probably will be the principal recipients of such programs, and although the adjuncts' teaching methods may be somewhat more anecdotal than those of full-time faculty, the adjuncts' "real world" approach may prove popular with the students.

Where should the emphasis be placed among undergraduate, master's, doctoral, and postdoctoral work?

The principal role of nonprofit studies in undergraduate education should be to expose the student to the independent sector, its important role in society, and some of the key challenges it currently faces. Such courses might attract students to the ideas and ideals of nonprofit sector work.

The heart of nonprofit management education should, in our view, take place at the master's level and with mid-career students. The topics listed earlier in this chapter are recommended for the master's level, and that level should be the point at which the bulk of these students are recruited. Master's students who lack career experience could be helped with internships and related programs. The doctoral level presents an opportunity to train researchers and policy analysts as well as a few scholars who could fill the teaching and research positions necessary to offer the master's level programs.

In several years, it also may be useful, in a *few* locations, to offer postdoctoral fellowships in order to provide activities such as teacher- and researcher-training seminars, opportunities to pursue new topics or reanalyze old ones through peer teaching/workshops, and, finally, a structured yet flexible environment in which a few individuals can pursue their own research projects.

Where should a curriculum and the program in which it is embedded fall along the continuum from "boutique to factory?"

We have staked out the edges of this spectrum with stark, value-laden terms to push our collective thinking a bit. We hope this device will help clarify a number of subissues within this question.

The advantage of the "boutique" approach is that it places little pressure on program directors to generate large numbers of students or field a large faculty. This approach concentrates on a small number of high-caliber students, includes a research component, and permits, even encourages, its faculty (full- and part-time) to do a fair amount of consulting as part of the boutique's program. Emphasis is placed on course quality via small classes, individually directed students, and substantial student use of courses offered by other departments. This approach could be particularly attractive to the mature, highly motivated, self-starting, and self-directed practitioner/scholar. It could also contain a very small doctoral program, executed on an Oxford, tutorial-like model with a heavier emphasis on mentorship. Such a program could graduate excellent students. One disadvantage of the "boutique" approach is that the small number of students involved will generate little in the way of resources to pay for all of the above. Also, the quality of the faculty must be superior to provide the sophisticated programming as outlined—again, with limited resources.

At the other end of the spectrum is the notion of a factory. Though we might have used a less pejorative term, such as "high-volume operation," we suspect that the reader will remember better the boutique-factory contrast. The primary focus of the "factory" would be to train a significantly larger number of students at the master's level. There would be no doctoral program and probably little emphasis on research or consulting. Greater attention would be paid to volume student recruitment and the building of a larger, diverse faculty including more practitioner-adjuncts who could handle the volume of students at relatively low cost. Some full-time faculty would be needed to carry out functions such as advising, supervision of master's theses or projects, and ensuring program continuity and quality.

Naturally, there are many opportunities within these two extremes. As we exchanged points of view with colleagues during the development of this chapter, we found a variety of opinions as to what was the preferred approach. Our own preference is for the smaller boutique operation with an emphasis on consulting, research, and a limited number of students. We also prefer attempting a dual affiliation with two or three graduate schools or departments within the same university, in spite of the many academic and political hurdles.

Is it feasible to establish a consortium of nonprofit management graduate programs across the country?

We believe that such a consortium is both feasible and important. However, working with several universities has persuaded us that such an effort would face significant obstacles, including reluctance of individual institutions to give up their autonomy, especially for a modest-sized program. The marketplace is ready, however. Graduate students, especially mid-career students, which may comprise much of the student body of graduate training programs in nonprofit management, are extremely mobile individuals. They may well be more mobile than the average person in society.

In order for nonprofit management education programs to be more market-driven, colleges and universities should strive to be less parochial and more flexible regarding transfer of credits, student transfers, allowing course work to be done simultaneously or in series at several graduate schools, reducing or waiving residency requirements, and other measures designed to facilitate student progress. Shibboleths of quality control and academic standards could be used to block creative collaborative efforts, but such collaborations are possible if key academicians and other opinion leaders push the notion further ahead.

Moreover, the opportunity to train and study in several different geographic settings, using some of the creative course scheduling tactics that we have successfully implemented with the University of Colorado at Denver, makes it possible for determined students to avail themselves of high-quality instructors in a number of different settings. The University of Colorado's doctoral "cohort" program, which utilizes intensively scheduled courses at campus and noncampus settings offered to students who currently live in a number of states, suggests that student mobility over a substantial distance is feasible.

Another benefit, envisioned initially as a possible approach for a system such as California's state university system, would be to allow member schools in a consortium to specialize and develop greater depth and experience in a particular subfield or specialty and permit students to rotate through several of the schools. A member school could still serve as the "home school" and a degree-granting locus for individual students while allowing them to take courses elsewhere.

8

Managing Nonprofits of Different Sizes

Jonathan B. Cook

SUMMARY

Almost by definition, there are major short-term, *operational* differences between managing a large organization and managing a small one. Everything from planning to financial management to fundraising is implemented somewhat differently depending on size. And, in general, managers of small nonprofits do things themselves, while managers of large nonprofits are more likely to get others to do things. It is neither easier nor harder to manage a small nonprofit than a large one, but it is different.

These operational differences due to size also affect the management assistance provided to nonprofit organizations by others. Consultants' diagnoses and prescriptions depend in part on their clients' circumstances, and audiences for many workshops self-select according to size-related needs. However, differences in the size of nonprofit organizations will probably matter little in the overall design or marketing of university programs for nonprofit managers. The required educational subject matter is not radically different for managers of organizations of different sized organizations. In addition, many of these managers will be seeking a career-focused experience that is not necessarily related to the size of their current organization. In any case, the economics of university programs will not support special offerings in the management of small nonprofit organizations. Aside from special grant-funded programs, the economics of university education dictate that assistance tailored to small nonprofits will be limited to publications, training, and technical assistance, primarily provided by people out-side the university system.

Despite the substantial operational differences, this author concludes that the primary significance of size in nonprofit organizations is *strategic* rather than operational. The strategic implications of an organization's size, and its decision about the size it desires to be in the future, are critical. The size-related strategic problems of small nonprofits are very different than those of large nonprofits and should be taught as part of planning and strategy formulation courses in universities.

INTRODUCTION

My first reaction to the question of whether it was different to manage large versus small nonprofits was: "Of course it is. I can teach a sufficient amount of basic bookkeeping to a small single-program nonprofit in a few days. It would take a few years to teach the skills necessary for adequate financial management for a multimillion dollar agency." And it seemed that other aspects of management would be more or less difficult depending on size.

On reflection, the matter got more complicated. Is it harder to manage a small, advocacy, membership-based organization with a surplus or a mid-sized, unionized nonprofit hospital with a major deficit? In the midst of my musings, I heard a voice say, "It depends."

My original questions soon started to lose importance to me. The answers to them seemed to make little practical difference to anyone. It does not matter much if big is harder or easier than small—if you manage either of them it is best to learn planning, fundraising, and other things that will vary somewhat depending on a nonprofit's characteristics and the circum-stances in which it might find itself. Nonprofit managers need certain fun-damental resources, knowledge, and skills in order to do a good job, and the need is nearly universal.

Then another voice chimed in: "Size makes a big difference!"

How can that be, I asked? The other voice said, "It depends."

And the answer came: "But the difference is not to the managers or in the management skills they need, but rather to the organization itself, and its ability to achieve its purpose. It is a major management and strategic issue, and the sad thing is that—most of the time—small doesn't work and big doesn't work either. In a nonmarket economy, it's sort of a Hobson's choice."

I did not like the answer and vowed to do something about it.

What is the implication of "size" for the management of nonprofit or-ganizations? This question raises a number of subsidiary questions:

Mechanical Questions

- Are large nonprofits more difficult to manage than small ones? Or are they easier?
- Does it require a different set of management skills to manage a large nonprofit than a small one? If so, do the skills vary for some aspects of management but not for others?

Educational and Training Questions

- Do educational needs vary for managers of nonprofits of different sizes?
- What effect does education or training have on the managers of large nonprofits? Of small ones?

Overall Effectiveness and Social Policy Questions

- Are large nonprofits more effective? Or less effective?
- What can be done by large nonprofits themselves to become more effective? By small nonprofits?
- What can be done by people outside these organizations to increase the likelihood that large or small nonprofits and/or their managers will be more effective?

This chapter addresses each of these questions. It focuses its greatest attention on the last set of questions, which—if the conclusions offered are correct—have significance for policy-makers and nonprofit leaders, and should affect organizational strategy and the allocation of time and money to and within nonprofit organizations.

DEFINITIONS

The definitions below serve to focus this chapter on public benefit non-profit organizations and to draw simple distinctions between very gray areas:

Nonprofit organization: an organization whose purpose is to provide a social service (broadly defined, so as to include arts and education) or solve a social problem, to or on behalf of the public at large, or some segment of it. Mutual benefit nonprofits are excluded from consideration here.

Large nonprofit: an agency with more than thirty professional staff and adequate funding for them from a broad base of support; an agency with more than $1 million in ongoing support from a constituent base; or an agency with an endowment sufficient to support it on an ongoing basis at its current level of activity. (Note that this definition places an organization with a small staff but a good deal of money in the "large" category. Large organizations, as defined here, have certain strategic similarities that outweigh some of the operational differences that derive from dif-ferences in staff size. The stability hypothesized in this chapter for large organizations may in fact kick in at a higher level than chosen here.)

Small nonprofit: not a large one; i.e., lacking any of the three characteristics that define "large."

Operational: relating to the short-term management of an organization and the *implementation* of its plans.

Strategic: relating to major directional choices made by the organization, designed to move it toward achievement of its vision. General usage of this word assumes that these choices determine the "business(es)" in which an organization will operate, and are made in the context of environmental and competitive factors.

The definition of size used here depends primarily on the source and amount of funding that support an organization. The stability, insularity, and relatively greater freedom from risk made possible by the three determinants of "large" are of strategic significance, as discussed below.

THE ECONOMY OF THE NONPROFIT SECTOR

Years ago Kenneth Boulding (1973) wrote of the "grants economy." His central thesis was that a nonmarket economy has a different logic than a marketplace. A corollary of that insight is that it is fallacious to rely on marketplace logic in a nonmarket economy.

In theory, the only reason for being nonprofit is to create a result that cannot be created commercially, or at least cannot be created well. Nonprofits should produce products and services needed for the welfare of society that the marketplace does not otherwise provide. If instead they produce marketplace products and services, there is no justification for their nonprofit status or for subsidy to them. (Services can seem similar and be different in important respects. For example, if nonprofit hospitals are correct in their claim that they provide services and serve constituencies that would otherwise be neglected, then they are in fact providing services that the marketplace does not provide.)

Subsidy is required to produce useful or needed things the market fails to provide (or to produce things at a lower overall cost to society, thereby increasing availability to a target client base that would not otherwise be served). Nonprofit organizations must meet this nonmarket test in order to operate in the public interest. Otherwise, they waste the scarce subsidy resources needed by other agencies. (Note that an organization that supports itself entirely on unsubsidized sales, fees, or admissions is not really in the nonmarket economy at all, even if its legal status is that of a nonprofit.)

The requirement that resources be generated in the form of subsidy means that one of two conditions must exist in a nonprofit over the long haul: (1) stable, effective fundraising, (2) endowment, including ownership of a substantial business (the latter is a form of endowment because it spins off revenues from capital that is not spent). These conditions generally require or assure (by definition) "large" size, and therefore long-term survival generally requires large scale.

The nature of small organizations in the nonprofit economy is that they depend on a small number of special people. Small is a fragile, unstable condition. Small is temporary. Although small business is also fragile, there are no stable nonprofit equivalents of the small family business that passes from generation to generation. When the initial key people move on, the "long haul" has reached a critical stage; the small nonprofit is now at even greater risk. Perhaps there is a 50–50 chance that the replacement leadership will not be able to perform at the same high level and carry on for very long.

Small nonprofit organizations, many using volunteers and/or a key leader as their form of subsidy, have produced some of society's greatest achievements and progress. But unless they then developed fundraising skills and connections after they lost their initial leadership, chances are they are no longer with us (which may be good or bad). Nonprofits that fail to grow become extinct. If small nonprofits do not go successfully into the donor market for an allocation of subsidy resources, they stay small and eventually close their doors. There are no "old," small nonprofits.

The resource allocation process in the nonprofit sector is extraordinarily inefficient, due to both its high cost and its deleterious impact on the results achieved by nonprofit organizations. Peter Drucker (1973), the closest we have to an oracle on management, has described the "tendencies to ineffectiveness" of organizations that acquire resources through budget allocations instead of in the marketplace. This principle applies to government too, of course, but—despite the differences in governmental and nonprofit resource allocation processes—it also applies to nonprofits. Gifts and contributions to nonprofits are budget allocations from individuals and grantmakers.

In a marketplace economy, there is a (perceived) equal exchange of value between a producer and a consumer. Goods or services are exchanged for money or barter:

Producer ⟷ Consumer

In the nonmarket economy, the consumer returns only part of the value received. The remainder of the value comes from the budget allocations of a third-party funder:

Funder

Producer ⟶ Consumer

(It might be noted that there are many value exchanges in nonprofit sector fundraising, and that a different kind of exchange, in which the consumer is not a participant, is taking place with third-party funders. Many of the size-related management problems identified in this chapter are compounded by the dysfunctional and inefficient resource allocation process in the nonprofit sector. The impetus for top management to focus on raising funds from third parties, rather than on product quality and organizational strength, affects both large and small organizations.)

The nature of the nonmarket economy is such that perceived "success"—both for managers and organizations—is heavily dependent on fundraising success once an organization has passed out of its formative years. This perceived success is an important ingredient in successful fundraising, which in turn allows growth and/or the maintenance of large size. Because of this, nonmarket organizations evolve toward *stable* scale even more than do organizations in the for-profit economy.

Later in this chapter we will examine the reasons why the surviving large nonprofits also evolve toward "tendencies to ineffectiveness" and what this means for their management and corporate strategy.

THE IMPACT OF SIZE ON THE MECHANICS OF MANAGING

In general, large requires more knowledge and experience, and presents more opportunities for "systems" to be beneficial. At the same time, small is every bit as difficult, perhaps more so because of the absence of systems and specialization. The technical management skills used in large organizations are largely transferable to small ones. The people management skills may have less relation to size.

Does Size Affect Ease of Management?

The answer to this question probably does not matter very much. Organizations doing good works come in all sizes. Their managers need to do the best job they can, and need the best management skills and experience they can acquire. Social policy setters should be concerned about the capabilities of, and management resources available to, groups of all sizes.

Larger organizations have more resources and therefore have more people to choose from when they hire their chief executive and other top staff. They tend to choose people with more skill and experience in either programs or management or both.

The staff of a small organization is personally responsible for implementing a wider range of management tasks and must therefore be expert in more things in order to perform adequately. Effective performance of many different management functions by a small number of individuals is unlikely to persist over a long period of time, especially following the departure of skilled or highly motivated founders.

There are many more small nonprofits than large ones, and a higher percentage of the smaller ones fail financially. But since the resources wasted are generally the volunteer time and limited funds of a few people, the loss is little noticed. However, the cumulative losses of the multitude of small nonprofits that fail are great.

All things considered, large nonprofit organizations are easier to manage. This is because they have the resources to hire specialists such as accountants, fundraisers, publicists, and so on. There is more at risk if the manager of a large nonprofit errs, but that does not mean that the job is more difficult.

Does Size Affect the Skills Needed to Manage a Nonprofit?

Organizational size affects some management skills more than others. Following is a tentative outline of the differential effects:

Little Effect: Large and Small Require Comparable Competency

- Planning
- Problem Solving
- Group Process
- Effective Meetings
- Legal and Tax Compliance
- Marketing

Modest Effect: Large Requires More Competency

- Accounting
- Resource Development
- Human Resources Management
- Boards of Directors
- Evaluation

Substantial Effect: Large Cannot Be Managed Adequately Without Substantial Additional Competency

- Financial Management
- Computers
- Information Systems
- Organizational Design

THE IMPLICATIONS OF SIZE FOR EDUCATIONAL AND TRAINING PROGRAMS

Do Educational Needs Vary for Nonprofits of Different Sizes?

At first blush this seems to be a curricular question, but it may simply be a marketing question for educators and trainers, and not a very important one at that. For example, courses on planned giving seem relevant primarily to large organizations (and they are in the best position to pay for them.) Yet that topic is sufficiently generic that small organizations can benefit from a course on this topic, even though they would be less likely to have planned giving programs. There would be no reason to exclude the managers of small nonprofits from such a course so long as they understood what they were getting into. Planned giving may seem an unlikely example of a course to be offered in universities (although by now there must be such a course somewhere). But there are few other examples of courses that would be of interest or applicability only to managers of large organizations.

Most topics, such as accounting, planning, and marketing, have enough generic applicability that they would be of interest to large and small organizations, although perhaps not to the same degree. Any organization that could use the skill would be interested in all of the same groundwork and much of the same advanced learning. Agencies and managers that would not use the skill would sort themselves out, especially if promotional materials indicate the conditions under which the knowledge is likely to be useful. Career nonprofit managers will in any case want to know how nonprofits of different sizes function.

So, from an educational point of view, it may not matter much whether students' current needs differ in modest ways. In any case, many of the managers being educated will eventually wind up in larger or smaller organizations than the ones that currently employ them. The Master's Degree in Small Nonprofit Management is not in the cards.

In a nonmarket economy, what is needed and what sells are often not the same. The early 1980s saw a new emphasis on "marketing" in nonprofit-management-related publications, workshops, and educational programs. Marketing was inappropriately sold to nonprofit managers as being the primary means of determining what products and services a nonprofit should offer. Using this method of inquiry, programs were in effect determined by learning what the client base wanted or by asking what the client base or third-party funders would buy.

For *unsubsidized* educational and training programs, effective marketing is indeed the right approach for determining products. *Subsidized* programs, however, while surely needing good marketing, should not be limited by it. They have a responsibility to think beyond the perceived desires of the client base or funders. Effective planning in a nonprofit organization determines *needed* programs and products, and marketing is then utilized to optimize revenues and participation. However, as suggested above, whether subsidized or not, university programs will be unlikely to use the size of the student's current employer as a significant factor in planning curriculum (although it may be a factor in fundraising and marketing).

If, however, size is a significant strategic issue, university programs should include course work on organizational scale, including some of the issues discussed here as well as subjects like growth, transitions, cutbacks, and mergers.

What Effect Does Management Education Have on the Managers of Nonprofits of Different Sizes?

The transferability of workshop learning to organizational settings is of course limited, no matter what the size of the organization. Training is a useful first step, but training alone does not usually lead to significant changes in organizational practices. Similarly, the effects of undergraduate and graduate education will be difficult to trace to the management performance of any specific agency. Transferability depends on many other factors.

Nevertheless, it seems likely that *any given training or educational experience will have a greater effect on the management of a small nonprofit than on a large one*. The manager doing the learning will on average be a larger part of the total management team of the agency, and the smaller agency will generally be easier to move and change.

THE IMPACT OF SIZE ON ORGANIZATIONAL EFFECTIVENESS

Implications for Long-term Strategy

The question of appropriate scale for the production of a variety of goods and services in the nonprofit sector is routinely neglected by the planners of programs and the allocators of resources to them.

Funders, the resource allocators, do ask scale-related questions such as "Who is on the board?" or "Is this a big-time operation that can pull this off?" But funders rarely analyze scale from the perspective of growth strategy, appropriate scale, competitive position, and cost-per-widget as contrasted with competitor costs and effectiveness—all of which would be mandatory before making a comparable for-profit investment choice.

Nonprofit founders and organizational leaders similarly undertake no such analysis. Years of their lives are at stake when they make their choices about structure and scale. They often make those choices in the dark.

The reason to "manage" is to make an organization work, i.e., achieve its purpose. *Effective* management moves the organization toward the achievement of its purpose, sometimes even at the expense of effective or efficient performance of the mechanical, operational functions of management. Purposeful, cost-effective results are more important than good accounting systems or well-kept personnel files. Efficient, expert performance of management tasks helps achieve purpose, but it is only a subsidiary measure of effective management.

Nonprofits, like anyone else, do not like to hear unfavorable ratings of their performance. They can be at least as self-congratulatory as business organizations. Often their pride is justified: nonprofits have contributed much to our national and international welfare. Many of the greatest accomplishments have come without much money—just people and commitment. But, just as in other sectors, for every example of greatness there are many examples of failure.

Large and small nonprofits are prone to very different kinds of failure. For a variety of reasons, most of which are inherent to the nonmarket economy, the "tendencies to ineffectiveness" are pervasive in the nonprofit sector. The "tendencies" are different in small organizations and large ones. Indeed, they are so different as to make organizational strategy fundamentally different in nonprofit organizations at opposite ends of the size spectrum.

Effects of Small Size on Organizational Effectiveness

The size-related management problems of small nonprofits include:

- Leadership turnover, leading to high organizational mortality.
- Inefficiencies of small scale. (Financial efficiency is possible, however, if volunteers are willing to be the organization's capital.)
- Poorer performance of technical management functions, due to the lesser degree of specialization (managers must play more roles) and the lesser experience and skill of managers.
- A (noble) tendency to continue delivering program services even when time and resources are short.
- Lack of sufficiently competitive fundraising resources and connections.
- Instability due to greater dependence on a narrower base of resources (board, volunteers, money, good will, etc.).

The effect of these problems is cumulative. Sometimes "success" is attained anyway, when offsetting special circumstances exist. Such circumstances might include:

- An idea whose time has come and which brings success in spite of poor management.
- The absence of competition for a nonprofit serving a local demand for personal services, such as day care or drug counseling.
- Wealthy relatives.

Small nonprofits are often accused of being so impassioned with their cause that they do not recognize the value of improving the management of their organization. But there is often an additional, rational reason for their neglect of management. With such a small program base over which to spread the costs of management, it often makes sense to skimp on aspects of operational management in order to optimize program delivery (but skimping on strategic planning, which is equally common, is folly). For example, an elaborate personnel system in a small agency may not be worth the effort.

Other smallness syndromes include the founder that won't let go; hostility to "management"; and extreme management styles (overly or insufficiently participative). But these are operational matters and by no means universal. They are of modest significance in assessing the strategic significance of size.

Effects of Large Size on Organizational Effectiveness

The size-related management problems of large nonprofits include:

- Inability to act quickly in response to opportunities and problems, due to such factors as cumbersome size, responsibility to diverse and sometimes conflicting constituencies, and donor restrictions/wishes. (It should be noted that this responsiveness to constituencies can also be a special source of strength and commitment to the organization.)
- Inability to change or act at all, i.e., fossilization, due to the power that special interest constituencies may have over the organization.
- Forgetting the purpose of the organization: losing sight of the interests of the client base, and existing instead for the prosperity of the institution itself.
- Higher costs, due to the relative absence of market pressures for cutting costs and working harder.
- Trying to grab all the turf and do everything, and winding up doing little of it well (the conglomerate syndrome), unrestrained by competition or countervailing political pressure.

The label "institutionalization"—reflecting organizations' desire to perpetuate themselves—may be appropriate to describe what happens to large, stable nonprofits. (A better label is needed, since effective "institutions" are necessary and desirable.) Whatever the label, the largeness syndromes are common, though not widely understood:

The Organization Prospers But the Clients Are Overlooked Except As Tools of the Institution. Example: The American university system. There are too many universities in this country. The ones that go out of business are those that run out of money. University long-range planning is focused on the survival of the institution instead of on efficient, quality education for students, without regard for which school provides the service. Proof of this lies in the fact that no university has ever, without being in financial trouble, gone out of business and turned its assets over to another university that could serve the client base better. Students are potential alumni, tools for perpetuation of the university.

Glamor Services Are Installed, Despite an Increase in Costs to the Overall Client Base. Example: The American hospital system in the 1970s. Before the phenomenon was brought under control, hospitals aggressively over-built beds and glamor services such as heart units. The result was overcapacity, which all foresaw. But none were willing to lose the battle for prestige.

Conglomeration: Many Different Kinds of Services and Programs Are Undertaken (Being All Things to All People, with Mixed Results). Example: United Ways. Unless the top management of a corporation knows a line of business, the likelihood is greater that it will not be performed effectively. In addition, managerial problems become compounded when one has to deal with diverse purposes as compared with the simpler circumstances of a single purpose.

Failed acquisitions outside their core business areas have cost American for-profit corporations billions of dollars in the last decade. Most of the business world has come to the realization that attempting to manage multiple unrelated businesses is bad business. "Stick to the knitting" sums up the recognition that a corporation usually manages its core businesses best.

The "full service United Way" concept, as depicted pictorially with a segmented, broad range of services for nonprofit organizations and the public, is a nonprofit analogy to this problem. Although primarily a mechanism for collecting and distributing money, the United Way has broadened its sights and now is in many cases a provider of services, competing with the very agencies (such as hotlines, volunteer bureaus, management assistance organizations, community planning agencies, and information and referral services) that it could instead fund to provide such services to the public. Being in both the funder and provider businesses creates a conflict of interest that compounds the effects of this conglomerate syndrome.

Opulence Becomes the Standard. Example: Major cultural organizations. It works for their fundraising, so they do it. Large arts organizations spend huge amounts maintaining their ambience in the style to which large donors have become accustomed. Serving as a social club for the rich is secondary to their arts purposes but is a necessary adjunct to successful fundraising for these agencies.

Employees Become the Living Dead. Example from another sector: Government agencies. Government agencies provide the classic stereotype of this pattern, but many large nonprofits have learned it too. Civil service and unionization of nonprofit settings are the most obvious signs, but they are only the formalization of practices that exist in many other large nonprofits too. At the informal level, demands for job security would be a good example of this pattern. In a well-managed organization, effective employees have job security. In a poorly managed organization, job security is a curse—somewhat like living out a horror story.

By citing universities, hospitals, United Ways, arts organizations, and government as examples of the problems of being large, it does not follow that these organizations should seek to be small. The examples were chosen in part because they reflect the mistakes made by some of our most valuable and important institutions.

But small scale is often not the remedy. And bashing the big guys runs risks of hurting their core businesses. In the words of Robert Greenleaf (1977, pp. 108–110):

Some of the criticism of our institutions has been addressed to bigness, as such, as a cause of their failure to serve better and, in some instances, of their positive harm. . . . On the other hand, if the power is dispersed through many small institutions, the service may be as poor and the hurt may be as great or greater, but there is no convenient single institution, nor a small cluster of them, to blame. . . . [Breaking up big agencies], . . . in the end, may create more problems than it solves, because it does not have the effect of building quality.

To summarize, small nonprofits tend toward all sorts of inefficiencies and failures. Their circumstances are somewhat like those of small businesses, but even less promising. Fortunately, they sometimes overcome these barriers and make great contributions.

But if those organizations choose to survive for the long haul, they must grow. The alternative, and often the best alternative for the client base, is to discontinue operations and apply the available resources in other ways.

Large organizations fail for different reasons, even more directly tied to the characteristics of the nonmarket economy. Their large scale is desirable, for it helps them achieve their purposes. But it insulates them from pressure to perform. (It does not entirely remove them from pressure to perform. Even the most susceptible of funders will eventually restrict their gifts in the face of truly embarrassing performance.)

The nature of human egos and relationships is that it often leads them to want more for their institution, rather than for their client base. But fund-raising "success" without true success is the biggest failure of all. If we do not like the message that neither large nor small nonprofits succeed, we must look for better answers.

WHAT CAN BE DONE TO IMPROVE MANAGEMENT IN NONPROFITS OF DIFFERENT SIZES?

For *small nonprofits,* the avenues for long-term improvements generally require increasing the scale of effort. The possible strategies for assuring improved long-term provision of services to a client base include:

- Merger
- Growth
- Cooperative networking with other agencies doing the same work
- Spinning off difficult programs to other organizations in order to devote resources to areas of concentration and strength
- Building up the strongest alternative organization (competitor) to carry on for the long haul
- Dissolution

Product improvement, cost cutting, and differentiation strategies are less promising due to the problems associated with small scale described above.

Short-term improvement is attainable through existing management as-sistance organizations, publications, and training and educational programs. For many nonprofits, smallness is an appropriate path. Examples of or-ganizations for which this would be the case are those which (1) have a purpose that can be achieved over a limited period of time, or (2) produce a result specifically associated with the talents, skills, or interests of a small number of people. Local activist groups or arts organizations of small scale are in the nature of things. Improving their management skills can always help the short-term performance of the agency, often in dramatic fashion.

Effectiveness and good management, especially good planning, have a high correlation, but they are by no means synonymous. To say that small-ness is temporary is not hostile to smallness, nor does it suggest that "small" is ineffective. Indeed, small can be the most effective scale, in spite of the likelihood of accompanying deficiencies in the nuts and bolts of manage-ment. In fact, the flip side of the instability "risk" to small nonprofits is that they are less likely to outlive their usefulness. Still, it is important that the planners and supporters of that agency understand the strategic impli-cations of scale.

Relying solely on better management techniques will not solve the sta-bility/scale dilemma faced by the typical small nonprofit. As discussed earlier, it is not even likely to lead to enduring excellence, surviving beyond the current leadership, in the performance of those techniques. (It should be noted, however, that even if becoming "large" increases stability in a nonmarket economy, the process of becoming large may have some de-stabilizing characteristics.)

Improving of operational management capabilities not only improves the short-term outputs of the small nonprofit, it also increases the likelihood that the organization will address its long-term strategic issues better. Train-ing, information, and technical assistance are the vehicles by which these organizations can improve their ability to make the critical strategic deci-sions.

For *large nonprofits,* the paths to improved management are more varied. No single strategic issue dominates their quest for better management. Improving their management skills and techniques will almost always pay off over the long haul. Thus, improvement of management in large non-profits is largely an operational issue. True, improvement of their planning capabilities could lead them to choose strategies for better service to their client bases instead of for organizational self-perpetuation. But improve-ment of planning skills is itself an operational question and can be imple-mented no matter what the long-term plans and strategy of the agency.

Fortunately, there is guidance available to large nonprofits seeking to improve their management, and in particular their planning. Such guidance must be actively sought out, for it requires caring and initiative to overcome the momentum of large organizations in a nonmarket economy. It also must be interpreted into nonprofit settings, because the best guidance avail-able has been prepared with for-profit organizations in mind. It often must be paid for. Some of the vehicles large nonprofits can use include:

- Education and training in long-range strategic planning for nonprofit organizations (it is not the same as in for-profits, because purpose, implementation processes, and many of the generic strategies are quite different)
- Decentralization of certain functions (knowing what to decentralize is much of the trick).
- Getting out of the conglomerate business. If more scale is needed, obtaining it through cooperation with similar agencies in the same or other cities is often a sound choice. That is now much the preferred and most profitable avenue chosen by for-profits, be they department store chains, automobile manufacturers, or fast-food companies. The logic applies in almost the same fashion to nonprofits (governance issues being the major distinction).
- The full range of generic good management techniques, which will always be a safe harbor for managers seeking to do better for themselves and their agencies.

These vehicles are of course important to all nonprofits, regardless of size. The immediacy of the prescription will vary slightly according to the circumstances of the agency, and those circumstances are often greatly affected by "size."

Small organizations offer individuals the opportunity to change society, provide services, and solve problems in new ways or in areas that are being underserved. Large institutions have the opportunity to assemble specialized talents and be stable, efficient forces for good in the society. Both can, and often do, miss these opportunities due to the failures of the people in the organizations. Some of those failures relate to scale, and in this respect, the strategies appropriate to organizations of different sizes deserve continuing attention.

9

Career Scenarios in Foundation Work

Arlene Kaplan Daniels

Foundations provide a little-known pocket of work opportunity for a variety of men and women from different backgrounds. The work is interesting, sometimes actually glamorous and exciting. The salary and working conditions are often optimal. However, there is really no systematic way to prepare for these positions; people often drift or fall into them. But, having found one such position, it may become easier to find the connections that can lead to another. The chancy nature of how one discovers the field, combined with the idiosyncratic nature of any particular foundation, produces a context in which a person may display personal aptitudes and interests. The field thus becomes an interesting arena in which the drama of career formation, development, and culmination may be studied. As Everett Hughes (1984, p. 406) noted:

Career is, in fact, a sort of running adjustment between a man and the various facts of life and his professional world. It involves the running of risks, for his career is his ultimate enterprise. . . . It contains a set of projections of himself into the future, and a set of predictions about the course of events in [that occupational] world.

While Hughes referred only to men (or the generic he), it is important to point out that as more and more women enter the workforce, both women and men make this adjustment.

In this study, we see how both women and men are distributed in executive positions within foundation work and how they use their understandings of the opportunities and resources available to each gender in the formation of a career. The data for this examination come from sixty open-ended interviews with a national sample of directors, program officers, and administrative assistants in foundations.

Foundations occupy a small but important area in the philanthropic sector of the United States. They include such organizations as individual or family, community, and corporate-sponsored foundations, the kinds of foundations that concern us here. (See Odendahl, Boris, and Daniels 1985, for a discussion of the types of foundations studied.) These organizations have a board of trustees or governors, who set the policy for grant-making, and a staff, ranging from one or two in the smallest to hundreds in the largest private foundations in the country. There is great variation, not only in number of staff but also in the extent of direction and control assumed by trustees, and the consequent freedom or limitation on the scope of authority delegated to the staff (Odendahl, Boris, and Daniels 1985, pp. 11–27). The common elements in the structure, however, are that a director or chief executive officer (CEO) takes responsibility for representing the foundation to the world and for the internal management and grant review, reporting to trustees who set the policy of the foundation, with or without participation from the CEO. The CEO may have program officers (POs) or assistant directors to review particular granting areas or to manage some other aspect of foundation business. These professional staff members are supported by some form of office-clerical staff. The chief among these are sometimes called executive secretaries but are often titled administrative assistants (AAs). This structure is supplemented, in various ways, by consultants hired as part-time or temporary employees, or paid honoraria, to provide such services as evaluating projects, providing management services, and writing state-of-the-art surveys and policy documents.

Although the foundation world is a small part of the economy (fewer than 5,000 people work in it), career patterns within it are interesting to study for their implications about development of a management profession in the nonprofit sector generally. The foundation world provides an unusual pocket of opportunity for those employed there, away from many of the usual vicissitudes of the business world—they dispense money rather than compete for it, for example. This context provides a natural setting in which to study employee perspectives on some comfortable work settings, with possible implications for nonprofit work beyond the narrow foundation field. At the same time, the limitations that accompany this opportunity show what difficulties may be present even in the most favorable working conditions. The opportunities and limitations, taken together, provide the sum of what the women and men in the foundation world talk about as they assess this field and their own career options within it.

One problem in this assessment lies in the amorphous nature of the field itself. The foundation world is small and subject to various external pressures: changes in the economy can affect the net worth and the consequent scope of granting ability; trustees may change the direction of the work; new government legislation may restrict or enlarge the capacity of private foundations to act in various ways. In addition, trustee governance may be idiosyncratic or even capricious, making it difficult to generalize about common patterns of activity in the field or even in one organization over time. Furthermore, people come to work in the field from very diverse backgrounds: from academic administration and university teaching and research; voluntary work and community organizations; journalism and advertising; corporate business, law, and banking; politics, government agencies, and social service. Finally, the field encompasses such a wide variety of organizations, of such different sizes, structures, and missions, that it is hard for employees to generalize, to see the elements that might unite them in a common occupation. The problem is compounded by the fact that many people are unaware that the field exists. Even many now working in it had not heard of it, much less considered working in it, before their employment.

Despite these difficulties, foundation work has a cachet for those who know about it. The work seems easily within the capacity of people from diverse backgrounds. One meets interesting and exciting people and has varied and interesting duties. Giving money away seems an agreeable occupation, particularly when joined with the notion of doing good, perhaps even being on the forefront of social change and social reform through the judicious placement of grants. There is little pressure for accountability from the rejected grantees and much appreciation—even flattery—from those accepted.

This cachet does not take into account the problems of foundation work: the difficulties that may arise while working with a capricious board or the status incongruities that may appear between board members and their CEOs; the problems of subordinate employees under a difficult or capricious CEO; the limitations on career mobility inherent in a very small field.

The following discussion of career lines shows how these elements of opportunity and limitation appear to the respondents with whom we spoke. (Interviews were collected by the three authors involved in Odendahl, Boris, and Daniels 1985. The selection principle for this sample is reported in the same volume, pp. 7–8.) The discussion presents some patterns that emerge in the histories of employment for CEOs in this study. In this review we see the interplay of past experience and entry into the field as they affect expectations and mobility within the organization. We also see how these considerations affect what career options informants see available to them in the future. Finally, we examine the larger issue of how career lines develop in foundation work and what implications this may have for development of management of foundations as a profession.

CHIEF EXECUTIVE OFFICERS

The CEOs of foundations are a varied lot; they come from very diverse backgrounds and serve very different types of organizations. They range from secretaries promoted up from handmaiden status to eminent former college presidents; and their responsibilities range from personal service for a family board, dispensing funds of a few hundred thousand a year, to large national and international foundations that give millions away. Despite this variety, some career patterns can be found.

One pattern shows the differences between men's and women's careers as CEOs. Men are more often CEOs in the large foundations and have higher salaries (Odendahl, Boris, and Daniels 1985, pp. 16–17); they more often have the more prestigious titles of president, while women are more often named administrator—a less commanding title than CEO (pp. 18–19). Furthermore, men more often sit with their boards of directors as voting members (p. 13) and are more likely to control discretionary funds (p. 23). In the following discussion, we look at the array of career patterns suggested by the experiences of the men and then those of the women CEOs to learn more about this overall picture.

The experiences reported by the sixteen male CEOs in this sample show four major career profiles: (1) the important figure from academic administration, business, or scientific research who adds luster to the job and to the foundation by coming; (2) the successful young professional in mid-career who may find this job a stepping-stone or a permanently satisfactory career improvement; (3) the man in a small or corporate foundation whose status is ambiguous and whose possibilities for promotion or further mobility are limited or unclear; (4) the businessman near or after retirement who provides the aura of stability or responsibility desired by his foundation and who finds the position interesting and also less taxing then his former career.

Category One: The Eminent Man

The important man who leaves a distinguished career as a university president, prominent researcher, or corporate executive to head a foundation is perhaps the most widely known figure in the foundation world. The events leading up to his selection and then departure from his previous position are often publicized in the media; the news stories and comments provide the public with some general idea about the activities of foundations and the functions of their executives. In this sample, four men fall into this category.

They come to their positions after illustrious, successful careers. One had, in his presidency, taken a major university through difficult times to a position of greater eminence than formerly; two had been high university officials with national reputations; one had been an internationally known researcher. They are all sufficiently senior to regard the CEO position as the capstone of a career and expect to remain until retirement. They provide direction for the foundation and give the impression that they exert some control over or at least give guidance for their board in setting policy.

Recognition of their eminence appears in the selection process, where they were courted and treated deferentially. Generally, they had not considered such possibilities until then. Furthermore, they expected deferential treatment and would not have considered a competitive effort for the job. The informal connections an eminent man has and the board's knowledge of his reputation indicate that these eminent figures are tied into networks that preclude the necessity for a competitive, open search process. Rather, the search process pays deference to a candidate's *amour propre,* suggesting that he is the only or the prime candidate for the job and that he will be courted accordingly.

These men all have the title of president, and they are voting board members as well. They preside over very large foundations with sizeable staffs and with millions to dispense or over smaller but very prestigious and well-endowed foundations. They are the final authority on the internal management of the foundation. They also provide the direction for the foundation policy. One indicator of their authority is their control of discretionary funds—up to $50,000 in one case. Another indicator is their responsibility to review investment policies for the foundation; still another is their control over the agenda—the policy issues the board should address as well as the array of proposals to be approved. Finally, these CEO-presidents give the impression of directing or at least guiding their boards. They have sufficient authority so that they may neglect their board members if they wish. In one case, a CEO regretted that he was too busy to keep them better informed. These CEOs also participate actively in the selection of new board members. This process is facilitated by easy, interpersonal relations with all or many board members. However, the CEOs see no need to curry favor or interests with board members.

These CEOs come with the power provided by the halo effect of previous positions. They are eminent and well respected in their professional circles. They add luster to an already illustrious organization, and their boards seem to be appropriately grateful.

Category Two: The Successful Male CEO at Mid-career

Another cluster of privileged, if not quite so powerful and eminent, CEOs is made up of men in mid-career. For them, the job is a step up from a previous job, or a promotion from within. They are now in small, prestigious, or regional foundations. Two of the six men in this group are also trustees with voting privileges on the board, but one had to insist on it at the time of appointment. However, one man refused this possibility on principle. "I don't believe in staff becoming members of the board of governors," he said. Despite this maverick position, the general view expressed by informants in this study is that voting membership is a sign of the power and authority of the CEO. A sign of the somewhat lesser power of this group of CEOs, then, is that not all are trustees as are the men in the preceding category.

Three of these men come from a journalism, political activism, and speechwriting background. One has also been a university budget officer. Another comes from a university development department with a background in public relations. The last man in this group comes from a background in community service agencies. The common thread among them, in regard to their suitability for a CEO position, is their contacts. Three knew someone on the board or someone knowledgeable about the selection process who recommended them. One man saw his regional connections as crucial. Another was unsure of his credentials but was persuaded to apply by an influential person in the selection process. In a parallel situation— when a political organization dissolved after an election—a director of a state service program was approached to apply. The general tone of their reminiscences of the selection process is of a competitive process in which contacts may have helped. However, two of the six men were courted more specifically, with the idea that they were the first choice.

These CEOs are also different from the previous group in their mid-career status. They are not clearly in the culminating position of their career, yet they may not see anything as desirable in a future option. In consequence, most are in a quandary. The peculiar nature of the quandary for CEOs in this group arises from the mixture of satisfactions and career ambitions that they express. Like other foundation workers, they like the flexibility, and their position provides exciting, varied work. They focus not only on the interest and excitement of the work but also on the opportunities for self-growth. Another common element is enjoyment of the work; the work is fun. Working conditions are optimal when you organize the staff at your own discretion. Some CEOs stress the social significance of their work as initiators of projects.

Under these circumstances, it is not hard to see why CEOs at mid-career might not feel compelled to make changes or actively seek new positions, even if the field were growing more rapidly and provided more alternatives than are currently available (Odendahl, Boris, and Daniels 1985, p. 58). They are really not under pressure to resolve their quandary.

Category Three: The Male CEO in an Ambiguous Position

The quandary may be exacerbated, however, for men who come as CEOs to small and regional foundations in mid-career and for men who move from positions in corporate business into that corporation's foundation. The three men who illustrate this category are all in positions that contain some elements of ambiguity thay may add to their quandary. They are comfortable in the work, but their future may not be as comfortable. One presides over a foundation with rapidly diminishing assets. Another is unsure of his future options in the corporation after directing its foundation. The third focuses on the delicate balance required to manage a small family foundation. Their problems are aggravated when adversity makes this particular foundation job less attractive. If one is spoiled for other kinds of work, and the current position is now less satisfactory, the lack of many alternatives in the field is a serious issue.

A variant of this problem arises for an executive picked from the parent corporation to direct its foundation. The future of a foundation executive is tied to the corporation. The career of a CEO can thus be an ambiguously valued stepping-stone when achieved in mid-career. (As we shall see, a position as corporation foundation executive may be interpreted quite differently by someone in a pre- or post-retirement position, or by women.)

Another variant of the problem arises from the balance maintained between board and staff authority. The club or congenial aspect of the work, while present in many occupations, takes on special significance in an area where specific professional talents are less important than congeniality.

One CEO suggested a contingency affecting the selection of women as CEOs: "The board members were simply not prepared to approve of a woman for the job that had so much authority." This principle of selection also provides an explanation for why women note the explicit powers of the board more often than their male counterparts: when boards wish to keep authority in their own hands, they may seek someone to do their bidding rather than to take charge; in such circumstances a woman may seem a likely candidate to traditionally oriented board members. Where traditional views and a wish for a CEO as director with more authority come together, a man will seem the likely candidate. Women wishing the titles and prerogatives assumed by men in parallel positions may find themselves in conflict situations with their boards. The use of power by the board, suggested in hiring practices, is sometimes supported by class as well as status differences between the members and their CEO. One officer mentioned the "retainer aspect" of his work that he wished to avoid. Implicit indications of the power of the board can also be supported by explicit limitations that circumscribe a CEO's activity.

In the foundation, the family [doesn't] want controversy or me running for office or in political campaigns. That or any hairy, community battle. It's a problem when the name of the family association and the members and the trustees are all the same.

Such circumscriptions are not special or different from many required of public servants or people in business. But their appearance in a context where board members make idiosyncratic or personalistic decisions in hiring, and where status–class discrepancies keep CEOs at a distance, requires them to maintain a delicate balance. A CEO makes efforts to "psyche out" his board when predicting granting decisions.

I never really know why we do or don't fund, but I am guessing better after seven years.

In this case, the ambiguities of the position are offset by the advantages others speak of also: the interest and variety in work, the generous salary, the absence of competitive and accountability pressures. Nonetheless, the future is uncertain for these mid-career CEOs whether they are in the previous mid-level group or in this one, which faces more ambiguity in the position. They cannot see any orderly progression beyond the position they now hold; most have trouble envisioning alternatives.

Category Four: The CEO at or Near Retirement

The last group of male CEOs has no such troubles. These three men are close to retirement or in postretirement positions. Consequently, they have no interest in future employment. One has just retired from a CPA firm; the other two have, after career changes, found the job from which they intend to retire. All of them had friends on the board or friends who knew the selection committee. Two of them were established and well known in the local community where the foundation operates.

The man who has just retired has come to a small organization (three on the staff). He views his job as a low-stress endeavor with limited hours, something of a pastime. He found his job through the old-boy network and got the job over eighteen applicants.

The other two men have been at their foundation career longer (twelve and fifteen years, respectively) and participate more actively in directing their organizations. One comes from a career in his own business. He works to shape the composition of the board and feels valued by the board (they had recently voted him some special perks in recognition of his service). Now in his sixties, he intends to work there as long as he is able and the board approves. Again, he got the job through the old-boy network. The work is not onerous; much of the administration—financial management, legal business—is farmed out to special management firms. The staff is small (three full-time and two part-time), and his wife works for him on a part-time basis when the secretary goes on vacation. The impression suggested by his remarks is, as in the previous case, of an interesting but low-pressure job with many rewards.

The third man is more of an organization builder (he now has a staff of thirty). He came in his early fifties to his second career from advertising-marketing. His current position is in a community foundation, and he has aggressively sought new donors as well as new areas to fund. He also actively sought a foundation position, desiring a career change; but he was courted as well. Like his colleagues, he intends to work into the indefinite future. And, like his colleagues in this category, he is pleased with his relations to the board; the members are attentive to his feelings. Furthermore, he enjoys warm relations with his chair.

The common elements in this final category of male CEOs are their satisfaction with their position and their desire to remain. This feeling is also the most common element in the approach to their careers for male CEOs generally. In addition to all the advantages of foundation work that any workers in the field are likely to mention, the CEOs enjoy the sense of autonomy and control that comes from the ability to organize their work and direct their staff as they wish. They also share in policy-making and, sometimes, board selection. Boards are often deferential to the wishes of their CEO; even when CEOs mention their own necessity to defer to the board, they stress the attention to their *amour propre* that board members are willing to give. It is not surprising that male CEOs have difficulty envisioning something better to warrant a change of career.

The situation is quite different for the women who are CEOs. As noted earlier, women are concentrated in the smaller foundations and receive lower salaries than their male counterparts (Odendahl, Boris, and Daniels 1985, pp. 16–17). Fewer of them have the title of president (one-third of the women compared to two-thirds of the men), and two have had to argue to change from a lesser title to executive director—only one successfully (p. 19). Finally, only two women CEOs serve as voting members of their boards, compared to six men.

This comparison suggests the differences in status that men and women find in their executive positions. The types of careers women report add substance to this picture. The twelve women (this analysis includes one more woman in the CEO category than is found in the study provided by Odendahl, Boris, and Daniels) can be found in five different career lines, only roughly comparable to the profiles reported by the men. For example, there are no women who arrived at the CEO position near or after retirement; there is only one (the fifth category) who is at all similar to the category of eminent men who bring luster to their position and are courted accordingly. Only one other category (the seventh) shows some resemblance to a male CEO type: that of the successful male at mid-career. But here, the women are mixed: from early to late in their careers. The remaining three categories show the clearest differences between women's and men's careers as CEOs: the sixth category is that of the unpaid volunteer to CEO.

The eighth is that of glorified personal assistant to the board, and the ninth is that of the secretary-administrative assistant who is promoted up through the organization to CEO.

Category Five: The Eminent Woman

This category—a person of eminence courted by the board of a prestigious foundation—contains one woman. Unlike her male counterparts, she has spent most of her working career in foundations. When the vacancy arose, she actively pursued it. She is also unlike her most eminent peers in participating openly in a competitive search. And she is different in having expected, quite openly, that someone else would get the job. She is like her eminent colleagues, however, in her sense of leadership and guidance of the board rather than the reverse. And she is like them in seeing her position as the capstone of a career.

The career of the eminent woman CEO, despite its resemblances to some aspects of the male counterpart, is anomalous in the foundation field generally, as in this study. The single case of a woman in this sample reflects the low members of comparable types in the field at large (Odendahl, Boris, and Daniels 1985, p. 16). Another anomalous case is that of the woman full-time volunteer who rises to the status of CEO. Like women in general, she is likely to be found in the smaller foundations and, as we shall see in reviewing further types of career lines for women CEOs, she is likely to have more limitations on her authority and autonomy than do men in equivalent positions. Yet the very possibility of such a career trajectory is interesting to consider, for the potential career niche it suggests is available, if only for a select few.

Category Six: The CEO from a Volunteer Background

A very different trajectory from that of others in the CEO position is that of the woman who has spent most of her working career as an unpaid volunteer. She distinguishes herself from the rank-and-file volunteers by her title and by the nature of her accomplishments. These distinctions suggest the credentials and experience that legitimated the rise to her current position.

I had been a policy-making level volunteer for the previous twenty years. . . . I hadn't worked for pay but I had raised a great deal of money, and had worked on lots of boards. . . . I thought I might like to work on the other side.

She was aided in her search for the job by the contacts she had made as a volunteer. Now she is the CEO (with the full- or part-time services of a staff of eight) at a corporate foundation. She carries some of the cachet and influence of her volunteer experience with her to the position.

I serve on [several important state and local philanthropic boards]. I had those when I came. Some [of these were invaluable connections to the corporation as public relations] they felt they couldn't go out on the street and buy. . . . I am very much the foundation's piece of visibility in the community.

This CEO reports to the vice president of the parent company, who serves as president of the foundation, and she speaks of good relations with her seven-member board. In her three and a half years on the job, the amount of money she manages has doubled. This position is the culmination of twenty years of volunteering, and she enjoys it very much. But she would like a higher salary, and some of her duties, such as writing the minutes of committee meetings, are onerous. These duties, and some of her public relations activities (for example, helping a vice president manage a party at the firm's headquarters) suggest that her position includes more handmaiden-like functions than are mentioned by male executives in comparable corporate foundation positions. Yet she is satisfied in the job, perhaps because she compares her career, not to these corporation CEOs, but to others from the volunteer background who are less fortunate.

Category Seven: The Ambitious Woman CEO in a Small Organization

The one category other than that of the Eminent Woman that shows clear parallels to a male career pattern (the Successful Male CEO at Mid-career) is that of the woman CEO in a small organization. Like their male counterparts, these women see themselves as appreciated and respected by their board members, given opportunity to influence policy, and with the authority to make decisions about, and administer the internal organization of, the foundation. There are three women in this category. The first is in an organization that has five full-time staff in all and a part-time bookkeeper. She was hired initially as a consultant because of her experience in developing programs for other foundations. Her first permanent position was as assistant director, and then she was promoted to CEO from a field of 127 candidates. She is like her male counterparts in having good relations with a small (five-member) board. Like her counterparts, she spends time on psyching out her board.

I have an idea of how each one of them is going to vote. . . . If I feel that it is a shaky vote, I will meet with the individual board members where . . . there may be a problem.

She cannot always guide them; but on the whole, she feels that she has great success. She has learned to surmount dissension and resistance on the board. At times the board members do defer to her recommendations. And she feels that she has made progress educating the board about the need to discourage the idea of grants that are board-initiated and then approved.

In a sense, then, this CEO receives some deference from the board, though she has to work for it. In her openness about the need to pay court to board members, she is different from her male counterparts. More deference may be expected from women—or she may be more frank in discussing these matters than male executives who feel uncomfortable in discussing relationships that contain overtones of subservience. She is also different in finding her salary a limitation and expressing a definite desire for another career.

The second woman in this category is also in a small organization (a staff of three), but it is attached to a corporation. Like the preceding woman, this CEO began as a consultant and was promoted up. She began regular employment as a grants administrator and then petitioned for the title of executive director, which she has held for two years now.

I finally said to the board, wait a minute. I . . . am doing things that . . . are very similar to colleagues in the field [with] the title of executive director and I have been with this organization [eight years] and this is the top administrative job in the foundation. . . . I had asked for the title change earlier. . . . No fight, it was just [that] they said they would put it under consideration and I never got it. So this was the second time that I had raised it and I presented more valid arguments. . . . I was amazed at how easily they said yes.

This discussion suggests a more subordinate rather than collegial interaction with the board. The restrictions on autonomy also appear in this woman's inability to change board procedures and refocus targets for grant giving. Although successful in the first major job of her career, the CEO has no defined career trajectory in mind, placing her husband's career first. She expects to leave when his career requires a move. Her plans are accordingly vague—perhaps volunteer work at the new location or more time at home with their child. In this regard, she is quite different from the men—and most women—CEOs, who give their career primacy. The women in this sample are more often unmarried or divorced and not remarried than are the men (Odendahl, Boris, and Daniels 1985, pp. 60–61). And so they are at liberty to, or must, give their career first place.

The remaining woman in this category is divorced. She is ambitious and successful and most resembles the successful men at mid-career. She works with a small staff (two) and reports close, cordial relations with a small, dedicated board. One difference, however, is in her selection for the job. Like many of the women in this study, she came from a background in foundation work, and she actively sought the appointment. While she persuaded the board to appoint her, they were slow to give her an executive title and expand the foundation. She began as grants administrator with a part-time secretary, and four years later her situation improved. And she has been able to influence the direction of funding. Unlike her male counterparts, she sees work in the field as underpaid—perhaps reflecting her own evaluation of her salary. On the whole, however, she feels that the board has been good to work for. She is also like her male counterparts in having stayed longer in one place than she expected, but anticipating some sort of eventual change, though to what is unclear.

While this woman is gratified by her career progress, the overall impression one receives from the women in this category is that they have some reservations about their situation. They see themselves as having advanced into their current positions even though the rewards and the consideration from the board are not always what they would wish. Sometimes it has taken time for them to prove themselves and attain the title of CEO. They are content and even well satisfied with their position; but this content is relative. They compare their progress from where they started, not with the more privileged position of their male counterparts who start at the CEO level and speak more often of deferential treatment from the board. These women certainly have more grounds for satisfaction than do those in the next category of women CEOs to be discussed.

Category Eight: The Personal Assistant to the Board

A common aspect of work for all four of the women in this category is that they work in very small foundations (in two cases, the woman is the sole employee; the other women are in organizations with five or fewer on the staff). They all work for boards whose members often make capricious and unilateral decisions, usually without consulting the opinion of the CEO. However, they all know that they have been picked to work in a quasi-handmaiden status, so they are either not outraged or else have grown accustomed to this status.

The first woman in this category holds the title of executive director, inheriting her title, after working for three years, when the previous incumbent retired. She started as a part-time grants reviewer. She and the then director were the only employees. There are now four staff members in all, but the president of the board is also the retired CEO. He continues to work closely with and, it seems, to supervise the current CEO. The six-member board is accessible and gives some attention to her *amour propre*. However, she is still trying to negotiate a better relationship with her current president and former administrative supervisor. This woman, while happy in her work, is limited in career mobility by family responsibilities. Her husband is supportive but puts his own career first. Consequently, she has the major burden of family and child care. At the same time, she sees herself limited by the nature of the field.

My limitations are that I am a specialist. I don't think I would be considered for any foundation except this one in [this substantive area]. Also, we all know that there are . . . few opportunities for women in larger foundations and I doubt that's going to change very quickly.

However, it is clearly a good position for a woman who is the second career in the family and who is grateful for the opportunity to work in the area of her professional and personal interests.

An equally satisfied woman CEO in the same situation (married, with responsibility for the children and interested in the substantive areas covered by the foundation's funding policies) is the director of a small foundation under the guidance of a board president. The CEO, despite little previous experience, was handpicked for the job by the president. The relationship between the CEO and her president is very close. While there is a staff of five, the CEO really functions more as an assistant than an executive. She takes no role in planning or setting the direction of funding. She holds private reservations about granting priorities, yet has no power to influence decisions. Occasionally, she finds the capriciousness of the board president irksome.

The only truly exasperating thing is sometimes she will say, "yes I'm interested in this, let's go for it." And I set it all up and then a month or so goes by because her schedule is very crowded . . . or even two months and she says, "what's this? I'm not interested in this."

But on the whole, she accepts the directives of the president without comment.

Despite this picture of subordination, the CEO is a trustee and has discretionary funds, some of them shared with her president. The mixture of discretion and subordination makes the CEO's position somewhat ambiguous. While she holds the position of director/trustee, it does not seem that she has the kind of authority and autonomy of men who have such titles. However, these are not the people with whom she compares herself. She is happy in her job and enjoys working with (and for) her woman president. This CEO makes some interesting observations about how the two women work together.

Her mind is working on a hundred different things at once and she's very apt to talk about . . . housing in [a ghetto area] and the next thing we're talking about who she saw at cocktails the night before. That kind of thing drives a man crazy. I often go to . . . the hairdresser and sit with my files . . . it's a wonderful place to work with her because there she can't escape. . . . A man couldn't possibly do that, so in a way it works very well.

These remarks suggest the unique way women can combine their business and other interpersonal relations and also an implicit rationale for a relationship where the CEO is more handmaiden than executive. A theme underlying these anecdotes is that women can work together easily without concern for formal relationships or maintaining a distance that allows deference to the niceties of status distinctions. Unlike the male CEO who wished to avoid parties that emphasized the retainer aspect of his relationship to board members, this CEO is willing to overlook or even participate in such relationships to promote the work at hand. The net result, in the CEO's eyes, is that the two women make a fine team.

The position of CEO has various advantages for this woman. She enjoys the give and take with the board president. And she enjoys the rewards. Her career concerns are also affected by the level of expectations a traditional woman comes to accept.

Another woman CEO also enjoys her position despite limitations. She describes her duties as bookkeeping and secretarial—as the only employee in a small, local foundation. She began as secretary and then became treasurer. After five years she requested the title of executive director and got it. Despite the title, she performs some handmaiden and personal tasks for the board. And she is happy to do them.

I make coffee and part of my job description states that . . . I will provide home-baked goodies for all the board meetings. I like to bake so I don't mind.

A married woman without children, she had worked previously as a CPA in a firm where she managed nonprofit accounts. She found this position by chance, and it has worked out as an easy job with no surprises.

Some younger members are coming on the board, and she has hopes for a less conservative structure in the future. At the moment she is satisfied with her working relationships with board members even though she cannot sway them. The current situation seems satisfactory, perhaps because, like the preceding woman CEO, she had no expectation for a career and enjoys the position chance offered.

The position of handmaiden to a benevolent matriarch or to an affable, patriarchal board of directors may have advantages. But where benevolence is seen as lacking, these positions are less satisfactory. Under such circumstances, the subordinate status of the woman CEO is shown in its harshest light, as in the example provided by the last women in this category of the personal assistant.

This woman holds the title of executive administrator. She has tried without avail to persuade the board to change her title to executive director.

She has also tried to open up the membership by limiting terms of office and requiring rotation off the board after a seven-year term, but with indifferent success. Although the organization has grown under her direction from a two- to a four-person office, and although assets have also grown, this woman has little discretion in the management of the work or the direction of policy, and she found it difficult to reconcile herself to this situation.

[Board members] think in terms of whether a person is worthy or not. . . . If they know the person, it can work one way or the other.

The CEO is also disturbed about potential conflict of interest in hiring the son of a board member as the foundation's attorney as well as with the way board members are self-perpetuating and choose their friends if vacancies arise. In consequence, the board composition is limited to a narrow segment of interests and skills. A further discomfort for her is created by the bigotry of one board member. She says it makes her sick to her stomach.

The difficulties created by feeling powerless to influence significant issues are exacerbated by the style of staff treatment from board members. Salary increases are slow and reluctantly awarded, and board members are patronizing to their women employees.

One of my [board members] . . . would call me "lambchop." And the one who has just been president . . . calls us all "the girls."

Even while board members are paying what appear to be exorbitant fees to their advisors (despite potential conflict of interest), they are stingy and controlling about office expenses. In general, then, the board members make it plain that the staff is not important. The CEO speculates that perhaps she is treated this way because she is a woman. It is not surprising, then, that this woman has been actively looking for another job. She has found, however, that opportunities in foundation work are limited and wonders if her age is a factor. In mid-career, she has now been at this foundation thirteen years—longer, she says, than she has been anywhere. Her experience, and that of other CEOs who wonder where they could move should they decide to change positions, suggests the limitations of these career niches. When they are pleasant, the problem of where one could move after such a job is more academic.

Category Nine: Rising from Secretarial to CEO Status

The profile of the women CEOs who serve as personal assistants reveals one aspect of the possibilities for a subordinate, even subservient, relationship for staff in relation to the board. The possibility of rising in the organization from secretary or AA to CEO reveals another aspect—including the possibility of overcoming many subservient elements in the relationship. The three women profiled here work in large and/or prestigious foundations: two in some form of corporate foundation and the other in an international foundation. Their career lines illustrate both the possibilities and the constraints of this dramatic rise.

The first woman shows a gradual but constant progress up the ladder within the parent or sponsoring corporation. She began as a flunky and worked all phases of operations to become an assistant supervisor. Then she joined the management development division as a trainee and ultimately became a public affairs officer. Ten years ago she took over the management of corporation contributions and four years later became a vice president. Five years ago she was named president of the foundation. She worked aggressively to shape the position of president and the newly structured foundation.

The [Corporation] Vice President called and asked who I thought should be on the board. I said I thought I should be.

Although she succeeded in this wish to be a member, her control and her authority are circumscribed by the corporation. For example, her discretionary funds are limited to proposals under $5,000. And she reports—as do most corporate foundation executives—both to a foundation board president and an executive in the corporation. Her discretion on staffing is also limited. The current staff number is four in all; she is hampered by insufficient staff but unable to change the situation. However, she has large areas of discretion. ("I write most of the policy.")

The opportunities provided by this job also provide a culmination to a long employment history in the corporation. A married woman with an encouraging spouse and no children, she has been free to pursue her career and intends to continue to do so. Although her salary is not equal to that of her male counterparts elsewhere in the corporation, and she would like more money, she is happy where she is. This picture of a capstone to a career stands in contrast to the eminent men in the first category of CEOs presented earlier, but bears some resemblance to that of the one eminent woman CEO in the fifth category. The culmination of a woman's career as CEO arises after a lengthy time in the foundation arena where she has to prove herself rather than being an appointment from another occupational category where she is already distinguished. The woman just discussed is different from the one eminent woman CEO, however, in the amount of active effort she has made to get, develop, and maintain her position. As a corporation foundation executive she is also limited in the authority she may exert and the scope of her powers.

The next case in this category shows us another type of career within the corporate structure. This woman returned to school and then the work force after divorce. She quickly rose from administrative assistant to division director in a corporation, managing charitable trusts. Under her direction, the division has doubled the value of its accounts and has grown from a staff of two to seven. Currently, she is a vice president in the corporation (the first woman vice president in eighty-five years). It is a competitive position for which she had to fight. Now she continues the competitive struggle in the larger corporation. She is ambitious and plans to rise, though not in this organization.

What I want to be is the director of a corporation and I want to accomplish that in five years. This [position] is a dead end as far as the company goes.

Her struggle for the vice presidency, and to maintain control once there, is part of a pattern—not just of the competition found in corporate structures, but of the difficulties caused by women's entry into male power structures. In her discussion of corporate experience, for example, she describes the delicate matter of executive coffee breaks. It is difficult to have coffee in the executive suite with a phalanx of officers who are close with information and visibly uncomfortable when she is there. And her efforts to advise and reprove an erring male officer are made more difficult by the inability of men to accept the same treatment from a woman as from a man.

I watched two higher accounts leave the company . . . over a relationship problem. An officer who always plays paddle tennis at 4:00 p.m. didn't want to go to an important meeting. I called him an asshole and explained to him how important it was for him to meet his responsibilities. He used that language all the time but became uncertain and shocked when hearing it from a woman.

She also notes that when her prior boss left the company, he was angry with her because she did not immediately quit. She doubts that he would have expected a man to do so.

The corporate environment, then, like other foundation settings, can present obstacles to ambitious women. The problem created by ambiguous or obstructive and even sexist behavior from male colleagues or superiors is a theme that recurs throughout many of these interviews.

The last woman in this category illustrates some of the potential ambiguities in the rise from flunky to executive. She has had a lengthy career in a distinguished international foundation. She found the job, when a young undergraduate, by a fluke.

I came as a summer relief receptionist. They wanted a student, someone who would work for nothing, practically. . . . I never left. . . . [I was] maid of all work. I did switchboard relief, mimeographing, filing, washing the walls, helping . . . move in furniture when they dropped it on the street because nobody delivered at that time.

Gradually . . . I was given a conference program almost totally to myself, helped pick out the guest list and follow the profession and cull the grants and . . . department rosters in the area to invite people. I set up with the caterers. I learned all this on the spot. . . . I was 18 years old and I'd never . . . even spoken on the telephone. . . . So I was really about as green as you could come.

This woman was lucky to arrive while the foundation was still small. As it grew, she continued to acquire responsibilities; she managed equipment for research laboratories connected with the foundation. Then she moved into analysis and evaluation of completed grants. From receptionist she graduated to project assistant, then project director and grants analyst. When the director died, she was informally running the foundation. After the director's death, this woman was championed for replacement by the vice chair, who thought she could do the job if she had a strong president behind her. At first she demurred. Ultimately she was persuaded, and she overcame a bid for the job by a board member, remaining director since then. However, her strategies for leadership have stressed traditional feminine tactics: dependence on powerful figureheads.

If I found being a woman handicapped me, I simply managed through a man. I found a man to use . . . as my beard..

Recently, the job has become less attractive and she has lost some of her authority. For example, she no longer is on the board of directors. And the board pays little attention to facilitating her work. She feels underpaid and overworked, as the staff has dwindled from twenty-one to seven. The board is also not sensitive to the problems of internal management confronting the CEO, or else it is indifferent to her wishes. This suggests that the CEO is not in a strong position, despite her success at upward mobility in the organization. There is little she can do to better her situation now that she no longer has the same free access to board members—and voice in selection of members—that she had when a member herself.

Now, later in her career, this woman is limited in mobility by her growing family and her need to support them while her husband engages in a career change. She is also limited by her own lifetime concentration in one foundation to the exclusion of completing her doctoral work or acquiring other work experiences and connections. It is difficult, but she is philosophical, realizing that many in her field with higher educational credentials cannot get work. The progression up the ladder from flunky to director shows a peculiar twist for this woman, reversing as she experiences setbacks, possibly created by changes in the board of directors and consequent changes in the lineup of support for her administration. Although her career in the foundation has given her some eminence, it is insufficient to provide leverage with the board. Her problems highlight an underlying structural problem for women in their rise through an organization that eminent outsiders who arrive as CEOs do not have. These problems are compounded by the traditional expectations and evaluation of women in our society. Assistance and facilitation seem more appropriate roles for women than direction and leadership. Positions as executives, then, are always filled with ambiguity for women.

The problems of maintaining autonomy and authority suggest a recurring theme throughout these interviews with women CEOs: their positions are structurally precarious. Except for the one eminent woman in the sample, these women are limited by the support (or indifference to their wishes) of their directors, on the one hand, and the available market for their employment, on the other. Thus, even when they are directors or presidents, the women's positions reflect some of the general evaluations of women and their work that are current in the society. Women fortunate enough to work with feminist or egalitarian boards are privileged; but such an opportunity is not an automatic part of the job. The impression left by the profiles of women and men CEOs indicates that the opportunity for autonomy and authority is assumed by the men but may be a rare opportunity for the women.

Underlying the preceding discussion of career scenarios for men and women is a sense of what the duties and responsibilities, rewards, and prerogatives of foundation executives ought to be. The more eminent among the CEOs have higher expectations; but even the more put-upon of the (women) executives show, by what they resent or tolerate, that notions of what is appropriate to the CEO role have been developing. As these notions develop, so does the idea of a professional career; an occupation can become a profession in this process. The following discussion shows how this process can be understood and how it has begun in foundation work. The discussion reviews the process of rationalization or "career straightening" as described by Hughes, the difficulties of this process in foundation work—exacerbated by the nature of board-staff relations—and the dim prospects for this process.

DISCUSSION: THE DIFFICULTIES OF RATIONALIZING A CAREER LINE IN FOUNDATION WORK

Everett Hughes (1984, pp. 363–472) has examined the general phenomenon of how members of occupations attempt to raise the status of their work and to professionalize, distinguishing their work from that of lesser occupations. His remarks are instructive for understanding the future of rationalization in foundation work. For, as Hughes points out, the first people to practice a new line of work come from other occupations and from various stages in already developed careers, as is the case for foundation workers.

In general, the desire to rationalize an occupation means that the first practitioners see a new need or a new opportunity, and so they develop the rationale for a special occupation. The next step is a push to require successors to choose the field earlier, follow a generally accepted course of study or training, and work under institutional arrangements that are defined and enforced by members of the occupation. At the same time, partisans for the new occupation try to build an occupational definition. They will look for committed recruits—those who enter early, get the approved training, identify with the collective activities of the occupation, and leave only to retire.

As the occupation builds its professional image, it seeks to reproduce and gain acceptance in the larger society. It expects loyal and enduring membership, and it presents itself as an accepted institution within the larger society. From this vantage point, the group can claim the mandate to select, train, initiate, and discipline its own members. As a consequence of successfully managing these moves, the professional group can define the nature of services to be performed; define terms for performance; and, if possible, extend the mandate to the point of monopoly, where others are excluded from the work and the profession can define the proper relations between practitioners and any others concerned in their work. The fullest realization of career straightening comes when the occupational group tries to develop a philosophy for society at large concerning the whole area of thought, value, and action involved directly or even remotely in their work. Of course, all of these steps presuppose regular openings, places for advancement, and opportunities for the newly trained.

This brief picture of career straightening charts the development of such professions as medicine and law particularly in the Western industrialized countries of Great Britain and the United States (Freidson 1986). They are the model against which occupations chart their own progress. The picture suggests all the problems facing foundation workers in any of their efforts to advance their profession as well as themselves in anticipating and developing career scenarios.

Foundation work is still in the early stages of occupation formation. As noted, practitioners come from diverse fields and arrive at various stages of already developed careers or from highly varied training. They are not overwhelmingly in favor of career specialization—many who arrive late in their careers, for example, do not see the need for any systematic preparation for the work and prefer the lack of specialization that permits people with varied talents and backgrounds to assume executive roles in foundation work. In any case, the structure of work limits the power of executives to set terms for their successors. The idiosyncracies of employer requirements rather than any universal problems of foundation management set the terms for selection. As the review of career lines has indicated, some major foundations need prestigious directors who add the luster from their previous careers to the eminence of the organization. Such directors are chosen to set the policies and direction of the foundation. At the other extreme, small and family-run foundations may want emissaries or even handmaidens to do their bidding. Whatever the type of foundation, CEOs report that boards of directors prize congeniality over specifics of preparation—and congeniality is defined in various ways, depending on the size and purpose of the foundation as well as the direction the board sets.

Such expectations create considerable obstacles to career straightening. The executives have the power neither to require a line of training nor to define and enforce conditions of work. These difficulties are compounded by lack of agreement among practitioners. First, there is no agreement about the essential training for the field. When asked, practitioners invariably suggested their own training and experience as a good background preparation. In consequence, there was no consensus about a basic set of requirements beyond a general college education, and some further specialized training (from any field). Finally, practitioners showed no agreement that their work created a clear occupational category or a career line to be pursued. Many of the older CEOs who came to this work after another career argued against career straightening. Some of the newer entrants—particularly those who could look forward to many further years of employment in the field—showed signs of interest in the rationalization of career lines. They form the mainstay of organizations and networks developing to consider issues of general interest to foundation workers, for example.

While there is no agreement about how to prepare for this occupation, or even if it is distinct enough to be called one, some consensus seems to be forming that a type of work has come into existence. The work is most rationalized in larger foundations which employ many assistant directors and program officers who have the opportunity to learn the scope and possibilities of work accordingly. Furthermore, external pressures from government and community agencies push foundations, whatever their size, to conform to public expectations (meeting changing tax requirements, preparing reports that disclose information about patterns of giving and use of assets, for example). These expectations require boards searching for CEOs to consider experience in these matters.

The nature of the work itself also creates pressures for stable, regularized patterns of work organization. Executives, particularly in large foundations, have a systematic pattern of internal organization and delegation of duties and internal specialization for the accomplishment of tasks. The bureaucratic form of organization conflicts with the more personalistic and idiosyncratic method of recruitment and assimilation of new executives by directors. The conflict can be resolved by a rationalized organization guided by the CEO, who then enjoys a more personalized relation with the board of directors.

Alternatively (and some of their subordinates among the program officers and administrative assistants occasionally praise or condemn this treatment), the CEO may run a foundation staff in a very idiosyncratic or even autocratic fashion, stamping the management of the grant-making procedure with his or her personality. Such opportunities occur, of course, only where boards leave internal office management to the CEO without interference. These distinctions mean that various types of managerial models coexist in the field. In general, CEOs report that they resist the trend toward bureaucratization and insist that organizational procedures be democratic and collegial rather than authoritarian and hierarchical. The reports of subordinates do not entirely support this view, however. Rather, it appears that some CEOs are seen as supportive with staff and open to their suggestions; other CEOs appear capricious and high-handed.

Efforts by foundation executives to begin formalizing understandings about their work and to set expectations for performance are beginning to emerge, however. These efforts appear in regions with sufficient concentration of foundations to support networks of executives. These networks sometimes include others (program officers and administrative assistants) from foundation staffs. Informants suggest that some informal powers—to recruit, train, guide, reward, or curb network members—have begun to develop. Members of a network may decide to "showcase" one of their number, for example, by electing him or her to a leadership position in the network and so providing visibility and contacts that may aid that person in consolidating or improving an existing position. Such channels for initiation and training are, however, particularistic and haphazard. Opportunities depend upon acquaintance and friendship patterns; no explicit, formalized system of application and entry has developed. Despite these limitations, recruitment and promotions can be influenced (though not controlled) by these networks. They can function as another contributor in the clublike circles through which names of recruits for positions are generated.

A serious stumbling block to the rationalizing of career lines in foundation work is the limited number of jobs. Scarcity means that those who depend on this occupation to build a career are hampered in finding options. In this way, foundation workers, like members of any occupation with a limited base and a very narrow apex (for example, fashion designers, movie actors, ballet dancers), find themselves in occupation where control emanates from many sources other than the practitioners.

Further problems for rationalizing their work come from some of the difficulties facing foundation workers that they may find hard to face. Hughes, in his essay "Mistakes at Work" (1984, pp. 316–325), points out that the outsider may have to show practitioners the problems that are difficult to face: "The outsider inquisitor lifts the veil from the group's own hidden anxieties, the things colleagues do not talk about, even among themselves" (p. 321).

For foundation workers, the most touchy subject would be relations with the board. The power of the executive is always limited; he or she serves at the pleasure of the board. Sometimes, as a few of the women CEOs report most explicitly, trustee action can be galling. More often, the power of the board may be masked by the compliance of the executive with board expectations. Where board and CEO work well together and understand one another, an executive may feel quite powerful and free to follow his or her own wishes. The women interviewed faced the issue of their limitations more openly than did the men; but for all, the lines of authority are clear. Very few executives have more authority and are more powerful in the foundation world than their board. In the nonprofit world generally, it sometimes happens that impresarios and directors of cultural institutions attain great power, but if they hit a losing streak—cease to create enormous popular successes—they can be overthrown by a board already resentful at the high-handed ways of artistes. Top CEOs of major foundations, like CEOs in many large nonprofit organizations, also sometimes seem to be as or even more powerful than board members. But there too, they are technically in the service of board members and can be replaced if too overweening.

The irony of the executive position is that it can involve a lot of power in the community the foundation serves, if the CEO is seen as one who influences the dispensing of grants. The CEO, as noted, may also wield considerable power internally, over staff. In consequence of these possibilities, CEOs seem to find it easier to focus on the dangers of arrogance rather than on the perils of having to court the good will of a board. In interviews, the problems of the work most often mentioned were the dangers of arrogance in foundation workers who may come to regard the money they give away as their own and so come to be capricious or arrogant in their behavior toward applicants.

Such fears point up the lack of a well-understood system of controls in a bureaucratic framework with checks on and understandings for performance of its functionaries. Both the possibility of galling (unreasonable) expectations of board members and the capricious (arrogant) behavior of CEOs point to the large areas of expectations in which there is no consensus about standards. Limited general understandings about what the work entails leave large areas of discretion—both to board and executive.

All these conditions mean that the career line is hard to straighten. It is difficult, accordingly, to foresee much rationalizing of the careers available to foundation workers. The work remains a highly idiosyncratic and almost accidentally discovered pocket or niche of opportunity for those who happen to come into contact with it.

10

Genesis of a Program: Management Education for Nonprofit Organizations

Mark E. Keane and Astrid E. Merget

Institutions of higher education have belatedly recognized a new professional cadre in our society. The third sector has matured well beyond the stereotype of its personnel and managers as volunteers and amateurs. These organizations are not only numerous but also range in size and complexity from fledgling civic associations to giants of national scope like United Way or the American Red Cross. By the 1980s their numbers, complexity, and unique mission prodded some professional and academic institutions dedicated to management education to take a serious look.

As national leagues of these organizations began to scrutinize the needs of their constituent groups, the caliber of management often surfaced as a critical concern. Also evident were the changing career patterns of nonprofit executives. In the past, executives emerged from the rank and file of a trade, profession, civic group, or union. In more recent years, executives of proven management ability were hopskotching from one nonprofit agency to another, often moving to larger and more complex ones. In short, "generalists" in nonprofit management were beginning to define a new cadre of professionals. This change was accompanied by a broader shift in employment patterns. For instance, the Committee on Placement and Internships of the National Association of Schools of Public Affairs and Administration (NASPAA) found evidence of a shift from government to nonprofit careers among graduates of its member institutions. In part, these changes were pragmatic responses to federal cutbacks; in part, they reflected the sentiments of many in the 1960s who abhorred jobs in big bureaucracies and preferred smaller, more informal agencies administering the public's affairs.

For the educators, twin philosophical and practical issues crystallized. Was there a distinctive body of knowledge to provide a substantive foundation for graduate-level education? Could such a body of knowledge be patched together from existing disciplines to form some coherent curriculum? This question in turn raised the turf issue: What department or school or academic unit should lay claim to professional education for the nonprofit sector? In short, there was a search for both substance and setting.

The present chapter chronicles the evolution of a professional education program tailored to a special segment of the nonprofit sector: trade and professional associations. Like all cases, its generalizability is limited, yet it may be illustrative of how programs develop around new career currents and new bodies of knowledge. The first part of the chapter summarizes the conditions that led to the new program. The second part outlines the program in place—its curriculum, faculty, and students. Finally, the chapter concludes with some propositions about the role of universities in nonprofit management education and with a list of issues critical to the debate over graduate education for nonprofit managers.

THE SEARCH FOR SUBSTANCE AND SETTING IN THE WASHINGTON SCENE

As teachers and researchers, academics pride themselves on being in the vanguard—discerning new knowledge and, in the case of professional education, finding new ways of applying it. However, professors are often parochial in view. Prevailing paradigms that guide research and demarcate disciplines often protect integrity at the cost of creative thinking. Universities institutionalize these tidy perspectives around departments, programs, schools, colleges, or other academic units. As in any institution, these demarcations can become reified even when obsolete or limiting. An example is the emergence of nonprofit management education, which neither business administration nor public administration departments foresaw.

The Scene: Nonprofits in Abundance

Washington, D.C., is a "company" town dominated by the federal government and the nation's capital. The president, the Congress, the courts, and the federal government agencies seem to eclipse all other enterprises, except for the lawyers, lobbyists, and corporate officers whose businesses feed off government trade and political brokering. Yet the city's second-largest industry falls in the third sector. Literally thousands of organizations, neither governmental nor for-profit, gather in Washington precisely because it is the capital. These organizations include members of the American

Society of Association Executives (ASAE), principally made up of professional associations and trade societies; Independent Sector, constituted in 1980 to give a united voice to voluntary and philanthropic agencies and selected foundations; the Council on Foundations, a national organization representing all foundations; and the "Big Seven," a group of organizations representing state and local government. Each organization in its own way voices concern about professional education for its constituents, the executive directors of the rank and file organizations. In some cases, the Washington groups have sought to meet needs internally. ASAE, for example, has had a long-standing certificate program with continuing education courses and in 1982 established a Task Force on Education to determine what knowledge and competencies its managers should possess. Independent Sector established education and managerial competency as one of its principal programmatic efforts and assigned a vice president to that mission. The International City Management Association (ICMA), which alone among the Big Seven was preoccupied with professional (nonpolitical) management of localities, began to chide schools of public administration—long the source of their professional managers—for poor performance. ICMA and NASPAA set up a joint task force to evaluate education for city managers and for managers of professional groups that speak nationally or statewide for their jurisdictions.

ASAE provides a compelling case of the move toward better management education. There are over 3,000 associations headquartered in metropolitan Washington, most of these associated with ASAE. The top leadership of trade and professional associations, both full-time and volunteer, is highly visible in the media and even more active in behind-the-scenes contacts with business and government leaders. Headquartered close to the White House, the AFL-CIO, and the Chamber of Commerce of the United States, ASAE works to elevate the ethical and educational standards of its members. For over fifteen years ASAE has offered a certification program leading to the title of Certified Association Executive, which entitles the holder to use the letters CAE after his or her name. The process involves education and training, activity in the society, and experience as an association executive, culminating in a written examination covering the basic principles and policies of managing nonprofit organizations. To maintain certification, credits must be accumulated every three years through a recertification process. Of the 10,000 members of ASAE, about 1,200 have achieved the CAE.

The certification program very effectively supports the institutional objectives of ASAE as a professional society. Unlike continuing education in law or medicine or engineering, it is not built on a base of required university degrees. It is intended rather to raise professional standards indirectly by encouraging attendance at training seminars and by recognizing the value of practical experience. The capstone examination is designed to test mastery of the body of knowledge; as such, it offers a promising opportunity for interchange between academic and practitioner viewpoints on what should be included.

As consensus builds as to what constitutes the unique body of knowledge, there is increasing evidence that another criterion of a profession is being met: the top association executives are being appointed because they have demonstrated capacity to manage an association rather than because of experience in the trade or profession represented by the association. Until recently, the members of boards making the appointments were more inclined to argue that "only an astronomer (or city manager, or car dealer) could understand us and realistically represent our business (or profession) to the rest of the world." There is a parallel here with, for example, the management of hospitals: formerly, board members were doctors and routinely appointed a doctor to run the hospital. As time went on it became clear that this procedure often ruined the hospital. Out of this appraisal grew the new profession of hospital administrators.

An increasing number of association executives who were originally selected from within their trade or profession are now concentrating on this as a distinct professional field apart from whatever career they may have followed previously. It is estimated that over half the managers recently appointed as association chief executive officers have come from management positions in other associations, moving away from the specific trade or profession where they started.

This important characteristic of a growing new profession gives special promise to new graduate programs in this field. More boards of directors are willing to look outside their own field to select a manager who can demonstrate through specific experience the capacity to run a nonprofit organization.

Armed with survey data on the educational backgrounds and interests of its members, the ASAE Task Force on Education examined course offerings in several graduate schools and attempted to match the educational interests of ASAE members with university curricula. The search for a match was disappointing. Neither the MBA sketched out in the criteria for accreditation by the American Assembly of Collegiate Schools of Business (AACSB), nor the MPA conceived in NASPAA standards, fit the bill. This raised further questions. Could a distinctive component for nonprofits be a specialization within either the MBA or the MPA? Or should an altogether new degree prevail? If the response favored the latter, was there an adequate foundation in academic knowledge, as measured by research and publications, theories, concepts, methods, and applications, on which to found a new degree? Where within the university would such a new degree be housed? In short, issues of academic integrity and institutional turf surfaced.

The Search for Substance

Analysis of the major unique characteristics of nonprofits helped clarify the substance question. Washington, as we have indicated, hosts a variety of nonprofit organizations, including trade associations, unions, professional societies, philanthropic organizations, foundations, civic and cultural groups, and various interest and advocacy groups. In Washington, many of these groups have a national perspective or are umbrellas for smaller local groups. State capitals would contain a similar set, whereas cities not organized around government would have a different configuration. In program design for a degree, locational setting can be a major factor.

In spite of the variety of Washington, D.C., nonprofits, certain patterns or characteristics emerged clearly:

Mission. These groups could be conceived of as serving principally either "private" or "public" purposes. For example, some organizations, while technically nonprofit, are in reality extensions of private, profit-oriented enterprises, as in the case of many professional or trade associations. Others, like philanthropic groups, are typically in service to community and assume a more civic orientation. The latter are partners with government, rendering services in the public interest. The former are extensions of private interests, sensitive to profit issues. However, the missions of the two groups seldom divide neatly on the public-private continuum. Even where the organization's mission seems public, as in the case of voluntary civic groups, the organization may adopt instrumental values of efficiency that resemble more the private sector. Nonprofit organizations draw on the values and ethics of both sectors, tilting now this way, now that.

Governance. Nonprofits are unique in yet another way. In larger ones, there is typically a full-time executive director responsible for managing a full-time staff, recurrent programs, and significant amounts of money in the implementation of policies set by the governing board. While the relationship superficially resembles council/committee-staff and CEO-board staff relationships in the government and business world, there are crucial differences.

The nonprofit board is usually made up of part-time members who lend their reputation, expertise, and resources to what they regard as meritorious or valuable endeavors. Their day-to-day allegiance is, however, to their own professions and positions of prominence from which they draw income or political influence. Their efforts on boards are typically voluntary. Neither the political nor the corporate model of governance seems to match the realities of nonprofit governance: elements of both are present.

Funding. The label "nonprofit" would surely seem to make these organizations more akin to public entities than private ones. But many nonprofits act like for-profits to generate funds for survival and program development. Fundraising is an essential element of nonprofit management. It requires a blend of entrepreneurial and political skills. Managers are increasingly called upon to develop, market, and sell services that not only respond to clients' or members' needs but also make money for the organizations.

Financial Management. The management of financial resources is of critical strategic value for nonprofit organizations. Lacking the coercive tax powers of government or access to investor funds for corporate ventures, these organizations may face precarious fiscal situations. Memberships can ebb and flow with the tides of a constituency, and donations often come and go in one-shot infusions. Planning and managing funds are prized skills.

Personnel. The degree of professional management a nonprofit can hire depends on size and financial resources. Many have but a handful of professionals; most rely heavily on membership involvement to carry out programs and projects. Volunteers, part-timers, and amateur managers are more often than not the "personnel" of these agencies. The recruitment and rewards are wholly different from the staffing of government and corporations. How to manage becomes more an art of leadership than an authoritative exercise in bureaucratic command-control systems of organizations. Teams, networks, and task forces are more likely the modes of operation except for the very large and more affluent nonprofit entities.

When nonprofits have enough money to hire full-time employees, managers have to design and implement more formal personnel systems. Issues of classification, evaluation, promotion, tenure, compensation, and affirmative action make it necessary to codify policies and procedures. The trappings of bureaucracy can sometimes threaten the team spirit cultivated at an earlier, more informal stage.

The distinctive nature of the nonprofit institutions in Washington, D.C., was a compelling indication that existing business and public administration programs would not be fully satisfactory. The nonprofits' uniqueness in mission, governance, funding, and personnel crossed both fields and even reached to others such as social work, political science, and law. Courses to construct a curriculum, however, could not simply be extracted from the offerings of several program areas without some mechanism for assuring integration. Furthermore, differences among various types of nonprofits demanded further curricular tailoring: associations can be quite distinct from civic groups and unions.

A curriculum for nonprofit managers, like business and public administration programs, must encompass more than an academic foundation. A professional education program must include:

Academic foundations

- Substantive knowledge (e.g., economics, finance, government)
- Methodologies (e.g., statistics, accounting)
- Normative perspectives (e.g., responsiveness, accountability)

Professional competencies

- Applied knowledge (e.g., budgeting, management)
- Skills (e.g., leadership, fundraising, brokering)
- Ethical postures (e.g., honesty, loyalty, legality)

Career paths

• Types of entry-level or mid-management jobs
• Long-term professional pursuits

Setting

The search for substance to support graduate education for nonprofit management surfaces the practical issue of the locus within a university for such a program. The preceding discussion suggests an interdisciplinary, professional framework for nonprofit management education. Yet the educational enclaves of schools, departments, divisions, and other units within universities often resist the new and novel.

At George Washington (GW) University in Washington, D.C., the leadership of the dean of the professional school housing both business and public administration along with several allied departments resolved the issue. Neither the MPA nor the MBA alone seemed a logical locus for two reasons: the interdisciplinary nature of the education straddled both; moreover, the accreditation or peer review processes driven by national standards for the respective degrees (NASPAA and AACSB) allowed little curricular latitude. The MBA was the least likely haven: courses on nonprofit management, if added, would represent only a modest fraction of the curriculum on top of all the degree requirements. The MBA degree requirements would deflect many aspiring nonprofit managers principally oriented to that sector. The MPA, while somewhat more flexible and perhaps more normatively inclined, presented similar obstacles.

The requirements for academic substance, coupled with the practical realities of marketing a degree and attracting students without diluting accreditation standards, all seemed to dictate a new degree designed by an interdepartmental committee. Each of four related departments (business administration, public administration, management science, and accountancy) seemed reluctant to commit faculty resources to the design of new courses either by taking some existing courses and adapting them to the nonprofit sector or by crafting wholly new ones. The leadership of the dean compelled the four departments to pledge commitment to design and staff the new offerings. The result was the new degree program, the Master of Association Management.

A PROGRAM IN PLACE

There were two distinct phases in launching the new degree program: developing the credibility of the degree within the GW academic community, and marketing it to practitioners in the community of Washington association executives. The process of designing the curriculum and guiding it through the maze of faculty review involving four departments required roughly three years. The degree was first offered in the fall of 1984, and a trickle of new students began to appear. By the fall of 1986, the introductory course had an enrollment of sixteen, and three other new courses in association management (marketing, financial management, and law and lobbying) had average enrollments of fifteen. The degree has been officially recognized by ASAE as meeting its criteria for management education. A $3,000 per year scholarship has been awarded by ASAE to one of the students, and a similar award has been made by the Washington area society of association executives.

Students

For the fall 1986 semester, eighteen students were formally admitted to the degree program. In addition, sixty-two students had taken one or more of the nine new association management courses. Information available from these eighty students gives a profile of people attracted to the program.

The data that follow concentrate primarily on those formally accepted into the degree program, i.e., those who have made the commitment to pursue the entire master's degree curriculum. When appropriate, some data for the nondegree students are included.

Nearly all the students are employees of mutual benefit trade and professional organizations. Examples of the trade associations represented by students include the Associated Builders and Contractors, the Automotive Dismantlers and Recyclers Association, and the U.S. League of Savings Institutions. Examples of professional associations sending students are the American Astronomical Society, the American College of Cardiology, and the African Medical Students Association. Some of the philanthropic, public benefit nonprofits represented are the American Recreation Coalition and the Conservation Resources Group.

All of these organizations are "charitable"; that is, donations to them are deductible from income taxes. None of them is a advocacy-type organization, and none is a church-related organization.

Students so far attracted to the GW program are typically:

- employed full-time
- working now for associations
- in middle management positions
- committed to a career in association management
- in their thirties
- taking one or two classes each semester in evening hours
- interested in a master's degree because they believe this degree will give them a special career advantage

Faculty and Curriculum

Of the forty-two required semester hours, twenty-four are in courses uniquely designed for managers in associations, and eighteen are generic management courses taught by faculty from the departments of Public Administration (PA), Business Administration (BA), and Management Science (MS). The eight courses (twenty-four hours) in association management are taught by a combination of adjunct and regular faculty. Adjunct faculty teach the legal, marketing, and financial management courses, while regular faculty teach organization and management (PA), computer and information systems (BA), basic required courses and capstone course (PA, director of the Master of Association Management program), and advanced marketing (BA). Since the six generic management courses (eighteen hours) are taught by regular faculty, a student typically will conclude the program with a mix of ten regular faculty and three adjuncts.

The body of knowledge courses are grouped in six substantive areas, as follows:

Marketing Strategies and Representation (6 hrs)

Comparative Institutions (9 hrs)

Communications, Media, and Information Systems (6 hrs)

Finance and Accounting (3 hrs)

Analytical and Research Methods (6 hrs)

Association Management (9 hrs)

These total thirteen courses, or thirty-nine hours, and the final course in the forty-two-hour program is an elective.

ISSUES AND QUESTIONS

The GW case may seem idiosyncratic, but may also offer some lessons useful to other institutions as they respond to the educational needs of the nonprofit sector. The remarks that follow address three educational perspectives: degree programs, university-based nondegree programs, and general issues of professional education for the sector that apply to universities and nonprofit organizations alike.

Degree Programs

The GW experience suggests several strategies for designing and implementing a new degree:

Opt for Diversity and Competitive Distinction Rather Than Homogeneity and Standardization in Program Design. As argued earlier, there are reasons to assert the distinctiveness of the nonprofit sector in terms of its mission, governance, finances, and personnel. There is emerging agreement on the knowledge and skills to be covered in a nonprofit management curriculum. But the variety of institutions in the sector, the recency of national networks like Independent Sector and the Council on Foundations, and the paucity of educational responses to nonprofit needs, strongly suggest that standardization, as evident in AACSB requirements for business schools or NASPAA standards for schools of public administration, is premature for the nonprofit sector.

Hence, a university should shape its program to capitalize on its unique position. It should work within its own institutional framework, intellectual endowments, and contextual setting. The GW program is not a model but rather illustrative of what the marketplace of universities can offer. The coexistence of business and public administration in one academic unit at GW permitted a particular kind of curricular response. Had either department been freestanding, the result might have been quite different; or had there been a school or program of social work, the coalition of interested parties and the resulting program might have had other academic accents. Similarly, the geographical setting was significant. Washington houses national umbrella associations; that slice of the sector seemed a natural target. Other settings—more densely populated by civic and philanthropic organizations with closer grass-roots ties, for example—would suggest an alternative focus. The types as well as numbers of nonprofits exert both a philosophical and a practical imperative on program design.

Mount a New Degree Program Rather Than Work Within the MPA or MBA. If the distinctive character of the nonprofit sector has legitimacy, then neither the MPA nor the MBA offers a suitable structure. Both degrees exhibit a parochial perspective on their respective sectors of government and business. The dictates of their accrediting bodies accentuate the disparities. Practical constraints such as limitation of resources might well dictate an interim solution such as a nonprofit management concentration within the MPA or MBA, but the student eager for education and a profession in nonprofit management would have to dedicate probably two-thirds of his or her educational energies, not to mention tuition dollars, toward mastery of another sector.

Select the Academic Setting of a Professional School Rather Than Arts and Sciences. The locus is crucial because professional schools espouse a distinctive educational mission. Unlike programs in arts and sciences, professional schools stretch their role beyond that of imparting the classical components of substantive knowledge, methodological rigor, and normative discourse. Professional schools emphasize the application of knowledge to practical problems, the acquisition of professional competencies among their students, and the development of ethical judgments in the conduct of their profession. In addition, the resources of professional schools often support their own complement of placement and internship offices, alumni networks, professional symposia, and continuing education; all facilitate the transition from scholarly student to practicing professional. Educators within professional schools frequently interact with practitioners over the course of their respective careers in an attempt to update and refresh academic offerings.

Convene an Advisory Board Composed of Academics and Professionals Over the Course of the Design, Implementation, and Evaluation Phases of the Program. Although the academic-practitioner interplay should always invigorate professional education, it is especially vital when a field like nonprofit management is developing. Schools of business and public administration have few, if any, experts in the nonprofit sector; yet the faculty do have command of bodies of knowledge that can inform the sector if adapted. Had the academics at GW not actively interacted with ASAE, the program would have been devoid of much of the content the profession deemed relevant; lacking professional legitimacy, it would also have had no marketing momentum to attract students and assure them of their career prospects. Just as the practitioners educated the academics, the reverse flow also instilled an appreciation of the larger corpus of knowledge—beyond the tricks and tools of management techniques—that leaders in the nonprofit sector should acquire. As a program matures, its alumni can become consultants in balancing academic integrity and professional currency.

Acquire Some Catalysts for Change. Money is a precious commodity for building a new program, especially where it can support faculty, but it is not the sole denominator. Resistance within universities seems inevitable with new programmatic developments spanning old disciplines and siphoning off resources. Leadership at some higher level is essential until a program establishes its academic respectability and its marketability. Often an asset in attracting the attention of academic deans or provosts is a constituency outside—vocal groups within the community, socioeconomic notables, foundations, professional societies, or whatever else may exert clout and conviction.

Target to Practitioners in Place Rather Than Recent College Graduates. Perhaps this proposition holds only until professional degrees in nonprofit management accumulate the academic solidity and professional recognition now associated with the MPA and MBA. A new degree is far more risky for a recent college graduate than for a practitioner whose career is already launched. As yet, the degree—whether GW's Master of Association Management or some other university's—has little visibility in the professional world. For a young person starting up with only the credential, the degree assumes greater market value in competing for a job; a new degree could be less portable than an MPA and MBA. Furthermore, a young person would fare better personally with not only a more established but also a more versatile degree than one so sector-specific where clear courses of career have yet to congeal. The pool of prospective students fresh from college is apt to be very small; there are few, if any, undergraduate feeders or catalysts. Undergraduate courses in volunteerism or citizenship are nearly nonexistent. For the younger student, an MPA or MBA with a concentration or electives in nonprofit management might be a more prudent strategy.

The more logical market is practitioners in place. The marketability of the credential itself is less salient, since these people can broker experience, not just education, in their career competition. Their pursuit of advanced studies is typically more substantive in motive than credential-driven. The intellectual appeal of graduate education in nonprofit management is not likely to occur until some years entry into the nonprofit world. Our experience suggests that for many the initial pull into the sector was narrowly construed: a concern for a specific community, charity, service, trade, or profession. Only some years later does a more generic interest in management materialize that transcends the particular mission of a nonprofit agency. When the concept of career overwhelms a specific job, then the kind of education envisioned by the GW program or other similarly constructed programs makes sense. The output sought by such a program—leaders and managers, where strategy more than technique prevails—pitches the program to someone already in the field.

As programs sprout, these propositions can stand the true test of evaluation and comparison. Until then, they stand purely as propositions, not prescriptions.

Nondegree Initiatives

Denominating an educational response to the sector only in terms of graduate degrees unduly understates the contribution a university can make to professionalism. The response of GW with a degree is in some senses parochial; it reflects the institution's educational flexibility, its faculty and financial resources, and its local market. Other universities will perforce be equally parochial. At maximum, a university can go beyond degree granting and course offering to become a regional or national center with research, technical assistance, continuing education, and conferences as its mission. Such is the model for the Mandel Center for Non-Profit Organizations at Case Western Reserve University.

At a minimum, universities can make more modest yet meaningful contributions. Faculty can search out opportunities to render technical assistance to nonprofit agencies in such areas as marketing, accounting, leadership, strategic planning, information systems, and so on. As consultants they could gain credit at a university for professional service while they apply their generic knowledge in the laboratory of a nonprofit organization. Continuing education programs can extend their entrepreneurial horizons easily with the flexibility and adaptability universities usually accord them. Student interns can help augment the typically stretched-thin staffs of nonprofit agencies. Many courses in professional schools are often client-centered; a project or study (be it in marketing or program evaluation) can be conducted at no fee under faculty supervision for a nonprofit. Increasingly, professional schools are fostering the academic-practitioner dialogue through exchange programs or executives-in-residence. In short, universities can render valuable service through their existing repertoire of activities in an effort to professionalize and upgrade the management of the nonprofit sector. What is needed to harness these resources is a better dialogue between a university and its local constituency of nonprofit organizations.

Crosscutting Issues for Educators

Issues that inspire sustained intellectual and professional energy will continue to crop up across universities and the nonprofit sector. Chief among them are:

A Distinctive Body of Knowledge. A good deal of the course work is plucked from existing curricula within traditional departments. For example, marketing in the nonprofit sector really may represent a traditional business course adapted by a few cases on nonprofits. Distinctive conceptual foundations, let alone cases, await more aggressive research and the formation of a literature. There is evidence of more research under way and more centers of intellectual and professional focus (e.g., the Mandel Center at Case Western). Yet the body of knowledge remains underdeveloped, at least conceptually, in such areas as mission, governance, financing, and managing people. Furthermore, is there a generic body of knowledge that comprehends the entire nonprofit sector, or should it be compartmentalized by type of organization?

Certification, Accreditation, Credentialing. The merits of these still remain controversial even in established areas like the MBA and MPA, where accreditation bodies armed by standards impose guidelines on degree programs and have currency in professional circles for employers. The nonprofit sector in its foundations for management education is too much in its infancy to promulgate guidelines. Even if there were the press to do so—at least for posturing academic maturity—could one set of guidelines span all varieties of degrees and all constituent units of the sector? What institution—existing or new—would lay claim?

Career Paths. With the recency of a self-conscious pursuit of careers in nonprofit management, the paths of the profession are unclear. Absent a civil service or a tradition of corporate promotion, how will careers unfold? How will effective managers become mobile across the pool of positions? Will indeed a new cadre of generalists in nonprofit management solidify as a profession? Should they?

For the decade ahead, these issues will invite dialogue across the universities with their professional organizations and the nonprofit organizations with their national networks.

11

Values Underlying Nonprofit Endeavor

Brian O'Connell

Few would know that efforts to create the organization Independent Sector came close to foundering at the very first meetings of its organizing committee. In bringing together representatives of the diversity of the sector, we gambled, and almost lost, that they would recognize their commonalities. For most of the first meeting and much of the second, they pronounced and demonstrated their differences to an extent that our mutual orientation was not to our likenesses but to the most extreme antipathies and wariness that separated us. Two years later, still sensitive and tentative, but with some understanding of common denominators, the committee concluded its recommendation to create a more permanent "meeting ground" with this observation:

We are aware of all the obstacles that stand in the way of the success of our proposal. Early in the Report, we deliberately underscored that "in the course of our examination, we have become even more aware of the overwhelming obstacles that have forestalled or foreclosed all earlier efforts to pull the sector together" and then we went on to enumerate several of these sobering barriers. But we also stated that "despite how very real these problems are and with full respect for them, they are nevertheless constantly countered by an impressively pervasive conviction that if the independent sector is to continue to serve society well, it must—to the extent possible—be mobilized for greater cooperation and influence. Despite all the differences, antipathies and antagonisms which may exist in this quarrelsome, competing and truly independent sector, there are even stronger forces pulling it together. However different all the other beliefs, there is a shared understanding of the sector's capacity to serve human needs and there is a shared stake in the fundamental relationship between the freedom of citizens to organize themselves and the freedom of citizens." (Independent Sector, 1979)

The turning point or, more accurately, the belated starting point in the committee's efforts came only after we began testing one another's underlying values. In that experience, we finally found our common ground. That experience was so significant that the body of the final report begins with it and with the values enunciated.

The independent sector is so vast and diverse that it reflects an enormous range of values. Using the wide-angle lens again, we constantly had to remind ourselves that we were dealing with the motivations and values inherent in such different institutions as garden clubs, schools for the blind, scientific laboratories and patients' rights committees. We are also trying to encompass groups that are sharply at odds with one another—the devout and the iconoclastic, those who are pro nuclear energy and those who are anti, and protectionists and free traders. One might argue that in the face of such infinite diversity, the Organizing Committee would do well to pass discreetly over the whole subject of values.

But, without denying the diversity of the sector and without proposing to set limits to that diversity, the Committee felt impelled to identify and state certain values which it regards as central to its own efforts—values which the proposed new organization should seek to foster.

The listing has undergone several changes, especially shortening, and now covers:

—commitment beyond self

—worth and dignity of the individual

—responsibility

—tolerance

—freedom

—justice

—responsibilities of citizenship

The basic human value should be enhanced by and flourish in an independent sector. Specifically, the sector, *operating at its best*:

—expands the diversity of personal options.

—represents a framework and tradition within which individuals can band together to pursue goals of their own choosing: free worship, joint citizen action and mutual pursuit of an endless number of interests.

—represents a seedbed for new ideas, new art forms, etc.

—gives people channels to experiment with activities and solutions.

—provides alternatives to government action.

—gives individuals an opportunity for a larger voice in how our society will function.

—contributes to a more enlightened electorate.

—encourages wiser use of resources. (Independent Sector, 1979)

Members of the organizing committee and students of the independent sector know that these values are not unique to leaders and institutions of this sector. The values are essentially those of a democratic society, not exclusive to nonprofit endeavors. However, most of us would probably agree that the *degree* of commitment to these values must be particularly strong in and across the voluntary sector's leadership ranks.

That degree of commitment will almost automatically carry with it a related devotion to maximum citizen involvement and influence, the messiest and most beautiful of our democratic processes. The nation is ambivalent about its pluralism. We want the opportunity to influence everything and everybody that affects our lives, but we do not want people interfering with us. The value of having some control over our own destiny, when multiplied by 240 million people, tests our true belief in people power. Most of us want to help people as long as we do not have to listen to them. The true leaders of the sector have a passionate belief in participatory democracy, including the multiplication of participants and the dispersion of power. These leaders enlarge and endure the democratic cacophony in order to hear the individual shrieks—and songs.

In the composite, all of the organizations of the sector represent the webs that hold America and its communities together. Peter Berger and Richard Neuhaus (1977) refer to them as our "mediating structures." David Mathews describes the nation as "Coalition America." Senator Daniel Patrick Moynihan (1979) believes that these organizations give people "outlets for outrage" and that "this helps explain why we are the longest-lived democracy in the history of the world."

Independence is another attribute of the sector that helps it to fulfill its values and, like commitment to active citizenship, is a value in and of itself. Obviously, no sector, no institution is entirely independent, but the sector does represent *independent* opportunities for innovation, criticism, and reform. Too often the sector is described in economic terms, with emphasis on the dollars and people involved in its service institutions, such as hospitals, schools, colleges, and social service agencies; these are enormously important, but emphasis on their direct services tends to obscure the even larger role and contribution of advocacy organizations. There are many roles that nonprofit organizations play, including providing service and acting as a vehicle through which the government fulfills some of its responsibility, but the largest contribution by far is the independence they provide for citizen action.

Speaking to the issue of independence, John W. Gardner (1979), one of the founders of Independent Sector, said:

Perhaps the most striking feature of the sector is its relative freedom from constraints and its resulting pluralism. Within the bounds of the law, all kinds of people can pursue any idea or program they wish. Unlike government, an independent sector group need not ascertain that its idea or philosophy is supported by some large constituency, and unlike the business sector, they do not need to pursue only those ideas which will be profitable. If a handful of people want to back a new idea, they need seek no larger consensus.

Americans have always believed in pluralism—the idea that a feee nation should be hospitable to many sources of initiative, many kinds of institutions, many conflicting beliefs, and many competing economic units. Our pluralism allows individuals and groups to pursue goals that they themselves formulate, and out of the pluralism has come virtually all of our creativity.

Institutions of the nonprofit sector are in a position to serve as the guardians of intellectual and artistic freedom. Both the commercial and political marketplaces are subject to leveling forces that may threaten standards of excellence. In the nonprofit sector, the fiercest champions of excellence may have their say. So may the champions of liberty and justice.

Most of the great movements of our society have their origins in this independent sector; for example, abolition of slavery, civil rights, public libraries, and care and opportunities for the handicapped. Some who led those efforts were viewed as unpopular, troublesome, rabble-rousing, and maybe even dangerous. One of our largest responsibilities is to keep open the freedoms that will allow their successors to establish the new causes of tomorrow. There is no greater danger to our liberty than allowing those in power to have any great control over their potential reformers.

At the core of the sector's being is the nation's commitment to freedom of religion. Despite how central it is to the sector's requirement of independence and the country's requirement of freedom, most discussions of nonprofit endeavor overlook religion altogether or skip over it as uncharacteristic. A proper perspective on the values and role of the sector has to relate to religious expression and the protection of it. As incredible as it might seem, we tend to get so preoccupied with other functions and institutions of the sector that we usually omit the churches from our discussion of voluntary activity.

In doing the book *America's Voluntary Spirit,* I was wrenched back to an awareness of how much of the tradition *and* services *and* advocacy of this sector relates to the earliest determinations of freedom of religion. We have tended to set aside that entire half of our sector as though it did not really belong, relating as it does largely to salvation, but if we look at what the conscience, the meeting ground, and the organized neighborliness represented by the churches have meant to the kind of society we are, organized religion takes on a different and even larger significance. We do not have to go back in history for examples. Who has been more in the forefront of the public business of the homeless and the resettlement of refugees?

In his *Washington Post* column of December 24, 1986, titled "The Vital Contributions Religion Has Made," David Broder quotes A. James Reichley of the Brookings Institution:

Religion and democracy will always be to some degree in tension; religion claims to reveal universal moral truths, binding in some sense on every human will; while democracy requires compromise, serving partial interests and accommodating differences of opinion that may appear logically irreconcilable. The two, nevertheless, have crucial complementary needs. Religion, as Alexis de Tocqueville observed long ago, is nurtured by the atmosphere of social freedom promoted by republican government. Democracy, for its part, depends, now and for the foreseeable future, on values that have no reliable source outside religion.

In a *Foundation News* article (September/October 1984), "A Metaphor Carried Too Far," John F. Wilson, professor of religion at Princeton and director of the Project on Church and State, took as his topic the separation of church and state.

We have also lost the subtle understanding of how religious groups operate in American society. As de Tocqueville saw so clearly, religion was the most pronounced strand of the new nation's voluntary behavior. It formed mores, educated citizens, and in general exercised a civilizing influence.

Tocqueville thought religion played this role effectively only because it did so voluntarily. This was, for him, a point of marked contrast with societies of the Old World.

We, of course, tend to forget that religion was in the 19th century (and continues in the 20th) the most pronounced form of voluntary behavior in American society.

Voluntary organizations have always represented our options and alternatives for doing things our own way or trying to demonstrate that there is a better way. Throughout our society there are parallel systems of public and private schools, colleges, libraries, museums, research institutes, recreation facilities, and day care centers. They are a reflection of our diversity, search for excellence, and freedom to experiment.

Beyond the urgent causes and crusades, the independent sector simply provides people with a chance to do their own thing—to be different—to be a bit freer—to be unique. Waldemar Nielsen (1980) summarized the variety of interests that Americans freely pursue through their voluntary organizations:

If your interest is people, you can help the elderly by a contribution to the Grey Panthers; or teenagers through the Jean Teen Scene of Chicago; or young children through your local nursery school; or everyone by giving to the Rock of All Ages in Philadelphia.

If your interest is animals, there is the ASPCA and Adopt-A-Pet; if fishes, the Izaak Walton League; if birds, the American Homing Pigeon Institute or the Easter Bird Banding Association.

If you are a WASP, there is the English Speaking Union and the Mayflower Descendants Association; if you have a still older association with the country, there is the Redcliff Chippewa Fund or the Museum of the American Indian.

If your vision is local, there is the Cook County Special Bail Project and Clean Up the Ghetto in Philadelphia; if national, there is America the Beautiful; if global, there is the United Nations Association; if celestial, there are the Sidewalk Astronomers of San Francisco.

If you are interested in tradition and social continuity, there is the Society for the Preservation of Historic Landmarks and the Portland Friends of Cast Iron Architecture; if social change is your passion there is Common Cause; and, if that seems too sober for you, there is the Union of Radical Political Economists or perhaps the Theatre for Revolutionary Satire in New York.

If your pleasure is music, there is a supermarket of choices—from Vocal Jazz to the Philharmonic Society to the American Guild of English Hand Bellringers.

If you don't know quite what you want, there is Get Your Head Together, Inc., of Glen Ridge, New Jersey. If your interests are contradictory, there is the Great Silence Broadcasting Foundation of California. If they are ambiguous, there is the Tombstone Health Service of Arizona.

So far I have dealt with some of the unique values of nonprofit endeavor and some of the unique qualifications or characteristics of the sector's leadership and have not centered on the immediate topic of management. Management functions and managers must, to a very real extent, reflect those uniquenesses even though day-to-day functions may not seem very different from any other setting.

It is my experience that the special requirements of nonprofit activity are sufficiently distinct that they call for a somewhat different degree and balance of personal attributes and professional skills. It is not so much that the successful individual has *different* personality traits or abilities than others, but that the *gradation* of them is different. I submit that one of the most important tools needed in the sector is a better grasp of the attributes and the skills most likely to contribute to personal and organizational success. With complete acknowledgment of that need, and speaking as a longtime practitioner and student of the sector, I re-submit the profile of successful nonprofit managers which I gave several years ago.

They're committed to public service. This is more than a generalization. The persons who succeed will face many rocky times. They'll be underpaid for their ability and they will put up with a great deal of conflict. For these reasons and many more, these persons must have a dedication to public service that will drive them through and over these obstacles and tough times.

They like people and get along well with them. Liking people is too often used as the only criterion for selection, and therefore it can be exaggerated. In carrying responsibile positions in voluntary agencies, however, most staff people deal with a wide variety of individuals and must be able to get along with them.

They can subordinate their personal needs and preferences to the needs and goals of the volunteers. This is among the characteristics that screen out the majority of people. Most of us cannot consistently subordinate our needs, aspirations, and satisfactions. But the really successful staff persons in the volunteer agency must have this capacity, or otherwise competition between staff and volunteers will develop and choke the opportunities for agency fulfillment.

They are flexible. In a voluntary agency there are frequent changes of schedules and plans, certainly sufficient to discourage anyone. Staff persons may be absolutely ready to accomplish a major task before the end of the week only to find that the responsible volunteer has completely changed the schedule or is unavailable to carry out his or her part of it. The successful staff person has got to be able to adjust and to concentrate on those tasks that are attainable.

They have a high amount of patience and tolerance. Staff persons work with a wide variety of volunteers who are often at their most excitable pitch. The more vibrant and active an agency, the more this will hold true. A staff person has got to be a stable and patient human being, or the emotional aspects of working together for significant goals will get out of hand.

They are mature. Psychologists define maturity as the ability to forego short-term satisfactions in favor of long-term goals. This applies to organizations as well as individuals, and particularly does it apply to successful staff persons. Most goals are long range and require persistent, dogged pursuit through all kinds of difficulties. The satisfactions are rarely found on a weekly or even monthly basis. It is only as the agency looks back from a longer perspective that the attainments are visible and the satisfactions present.

They are willing to work hard. Successful people usually work hard, and this is particularly true in the voluntary agency field. There is so very much to be done, the dedication of the volunteers is so high, and the number of forces to be dealt with so great that the only way to achieve success is by working awfully hard (O'Connell, 1976, pp. 40–41).

Just as with values and leadership characteristics, I readily acknowledge that such a profile is not unique to nonprofit managers, but I believe that these attributes must be particularly strong among them. I also acknowledge that the mission and function of various organizations will call upon different matches with my profile and that scale is a very real factor. But with full awareness of all the variables and exceptions, I am persuaded that the distinctions are sufficiently important to require attention in screening and developing nonprofit managers.

Some may feel that I am describing the best of the leaders of the sector but hardly the average. Perhaps, but we must find ways to identify and develop more of the best. We will not get very far if we assume that the values I have described do not apply to most of those we are trying to reach and therefore should not be emphasized. I would rather start with the quintessential values and help people identify with and reach for them.

Though we must be careful not to exaggerate the worth of voluntary activity, we must also not be unduly shy about helping people to realize what this sector means to our empowerment as people and freedom as a nation. Robert Lynn of the Lilly Endowment says it is his view and that of his foundation that "the independent or third sector represents the buffer area between government and the marketplace, where there is a celebration of America's values" (statement made orally at committee meeting). Students and leaders alike must be helped to share in that celebration even when the immediate tasks do not seem usual.

Appendix: Hosts, Presenters, and Participants at the Conference

HOSTS

Michael O'Neill, Director, Institute for Nonprofit Organization Management, University of San Francisco

Arthur L. Singer, Jr., Vice President, Alfred P. Sloan Foundation

Harry Weiner, Consultant, Alfred P. Sloan Foundation

Dennis R. Young, Professor, W. Averell Harriman College, State University of New York at Stony Brook

PRESENTERS

Jonathan B. Cook, National Executive Director, Support Centers of America

Richard M. Cyert, President, Carnegie-Mellon University

Arlene Kaplan Daniels, Professor of Sociology, Northwestern University

Paul J. DiMaggio, Executive Director, Program on Non-Profit Organizations, Institution for Social and Policy Studies, Yale University

Mark E. Keane, Distinguished Visiting Professor, Department of Public Administration, George Washington University

Robert F. Leduc, President, Institute for Nonprofit Organization Management, Denver

Reynold Levy, President, AT&T Foundation

Terry W. McAdam, Executive Vice President and Program Director, Conrad N. Hilton Foundation

Astrid E. Merget, Director and Professor, School of Public Administration, Ohio State University

Brian O'Connell, President, Independent Sector

Simon Slavin, Professor and founding Dean Emeritus, School of Social Administration, Temple University

Bruce C. Vladeck, President, United Hospital Fund

PARTICIPANTS

Carol L. Barbeito, President, Technical Assistance Center, Denver

Bertram Beck, Professor, Graduate School of Social Service, Fordham University, New York

David Billis, Professor, Programme of Research and Training into Voluntary Action, Brunel University, Middlesex, England

Arthur Blum, Acting Director, Mandell Center for Non-Profit Organizations, Case Western Reserve University, Cleveland, Ohio

Jerry Cronin, President, Independent Community Consultants, Hampton, Arkansas

Robert Curvin, Dean and Professor, Graduate School of Management and Urban Professions, New School for Social Research, New York

Peter R. Ellis, Program Director, W. K. Kellogg Foundation, Battle Creek, Michigan

Gregory R. Farrell, Executive Director, Fund for the City of New York

Francesca Gardner, Program Officer, The James Irvine Foundation, San Francisco

Susan B. Gould, Director, Public Management Program, Graduate School of Business, Stanford University

Sandra T. Gray, Vice President for Effective Sector Leadership/Management, Independent Sector, Washington, D.C.

Robert D. Herman, Associate Professor of Organizational Behavior, School of Business and Public Administration, University of Missouri—Kansas City

Antonia Hernandez, President and General Counsel, Mexican American Legal Defense and Educational Fund, Los Angeles

Charles A. Johnson, Vice President, Lilly Endowment, Inc., Indianapolis

Alan Kumamoto, President and Executive Director, Southern California Center for Nonprofit Management, Los Angeles

Leslie L. Luttgens, civic leader, San Francisco

Brooke W. Mahoney, Director, Volunteer Consulting Group, New York

David E. Mason, President, Supportive Services, New Orleans

Karl Mathiasen III, Founding Director, Management Assistance Group, Washington, D.C.

Nancy Meier, Director, Business Volunteers for the Arts, San Francisco Chamber of Commerce

Henry M. Mestre, Jr., Principal, XECORP, San Leandro, California

Mel Moyer, Professor and Co-Director, Voluntary Sector Management Program, Faculty of Administrative Studies, York University, Toronto

Arthur Naparstek, Dean, School of Applied Social Sciences, Case Western Reserve University, Cleveland

Martin A. Paley, Director, The San Francisco Foundation

William C. Pendleton, Consultant, Ford Foundation, New York

Donald L. Plambeck, Director, Volunteer Development Extension Program, Virginia Polytechnic Institute and State University, Falls Church, Virginia

Skip Rhodes, Manager, Contributions, Chevron USA, San Francisco

Geri Rivard, Program Officer, The David and Lucile Packard Foundation, Los Altos, California

Thomas J. Savage, S.J., Assistant Academic Vice President, Fairfield University, Fairfield, Connecticut

Benjamin R. Shute, Jr., Corporate Secretary, Rockefeller Brothers Fund, New York

Edward Skloot, President, New Business Ventures for Not-for-Profit Organizations, New York

Eugene R. Tempel, Vice President, Indiana University Foundation, Indianapolis

Jon Van Til, Associate Professor and Chair, Department of Urban Studies, Rutgers University, Camden, New Jersey

Robert Weiss, Executive Director, Center for Nonprofit Management, Dallas

George Wilkinson, Group Executive, United Way of America, Alexandria, Virginia

Kirke Wilson, Executive Director, Rosenberg Foundation, San Francisco

References

Abernathy, Robert H., & Hayes, William J. Managing our way to economic decline. *Harvard Business Review,* 1980, *58* (July–August), 67–77.

Barnard, Chester I. *The functions of the executive.* Cambridge, Mass.: Harvard University Press, 1938.

Bastable, C. W. Collegiate accounting needs re-evaluation. *Journal of Accountancy,* 1973, *136* (December), 51–57.

Baumol, William J., & Quandt, Richard E. Rules of thumb and optimally imperfect decisions. *American Economic Review,* 1964, *54* (2, I, March), 23–46.

Berger, Peter L., & Neuhaus, Richard J. *To empower people: The role of mediating structures in public policy.* Washington, D.C.: The American Enterprise Institute for Public Policy Research, 1977.

Billis, David. *Welfare bureaucracies: Their design and changes in response to social problems.* London: Heinemann Educational Books, 1984.

Blau, Peter M. A formal theory of differentiation in organizations. *American Sociological Review,* 1970, *35* (2), 201–218.

Boulding, Kenneth E. *The economy of love and fear: A preface to grants economics.* Belmont, Calif.: Wadsworth, 1973.

Butter, Irene H., Carpenter, Eugenia S., Kay, Bonnie J., & Simmons, Ruth S. Gender hierarchies in the health labor force. *International Journal of Health Services,* 1987, *17* (1), 133–149.

Chandler, Alfred D., Jr. *Strategy and structure: Chapters in the history of the American industrial enterprise.* Garden City, N.Y.: Doubleday, 1966.

Charnes, A., & Stedry, A. Exploratory models in the theory of budget control. In W. W. Cooper, H. J. Leavitt, & M. W. Shelly II (Eds.), *New perspectives in organization research* (pp. 212–249). New York: John Wiley & Sons, 1964.

Cohen, Michael D., & March, James G. *Leadership and ambiguity: The American college president.* New York: McGraw-Hill, 1974.

Coleman, Laurence Vail. *The museum in America: A critical study*. Washington, D.C.: The American Association of Museums, 1939.

Cyert, Richard M., & March, James G. *A behavioral theory of the firm*. Englewood Cliffs, N.J.: Prentice-Hall, 1963.

Dayton, Kenneth N. Governance is governance. *Professional Forum II Proceedings*. Washington, D.C.: Independent Sector, May 1985.

DeGroot, Morris H. *Optimal statistical decisions*. New York: McGraw-Hill, 1970.

DiMaggio, Paul. Can culture survive the marketplace? Working Paper No. 2062, Institution for Social and Policy Studies, Yale University, January 1983.

———. (Ed.). *Nonprofit enterprise in the arts: Studies in mission and constraint*. New York: Oxford University Press, 1986.

———. *Managers of the arts: The careers and opinions of administrators of U.S. art museums, resident theatres, orchestras and local arts agencies*. Washington, D.C.: Seven Locks Press, 1987.

———, & Powell, Walter J. The iron cage revisited: Institutional isomorphism and collective rationality in organizational fields. *American Sociological Review*, 1983, *48* (2), 147–160.

Disney, Diane M., Kimmich, Madeleine H., & Musselwhite, James C. *Partners in public service: Government and the nonprofit sector in Rhode Island*. Washington, D.C.: Urban Institute Press, 1984.

Drucker, Peter F. Managing the public service institution. *The Public Interest*, 1973, *33*, 43–60.

Dubin, Robert, & Taveggia, Thomas C. *The teaching-learning paradox: A comparative analysis of college teaching methods*. Eugene, Ore.: University of Oregon Press, 1968.

Fottler, Myron D. Is management really generic? *Academy of Management Review*, 1981, *6* (1), 1–12.

Freidson, Eliot. *Professional powers: A study of the institutionalization of formal knowledge*. Chicago: University of Chicago Press, 1986.

Gardner, John W. Keynote address, Council on Foundations annual meeting, Seattle, Wash., 1979.

Giamatti, A. Bartlett. Address to Yale class of 1960, 25th reunion. Excerpted in "A sample of A. Bartlett's quotations," *Yale Alumni Magazine*, June 1986, p. 31.

Gilbert, Neil. The commercialization of social welfare. *Journal of Applied Behavioral Science*, 1985, *21* (4), 365–376.

Goldner, Fred H., & Ritti, R. R. Professionalization as career immobility. *American Journal of Sociology*, 1967, *72* (5), 489–502.

Gray, Sandra T. *An independent sector resource directory of education and training opportunities and other services (2nd ed.)*. Washington, D.C.: Independent Sector, 1987.

Greenleaf, Robert K. *Servant leadership: A journey into the nature of legitimate power and greatness*. New York: Paulist Press, 1977.

Grossman, David A., Salamon, Lester M., & Altschuler, David M. *The New York nonprofit sector in a time of government retrenchment*. Washington, D.C.: Urban Institute Press, 1986.

Hansmann, Henry B. The role of nonprofit enterprise. *The Yale Law Journal*, 1980, *89* (April), 835–901.

Harder, W. Paul, Kimmich, Madeleine H., & Salamon, Lester M. *The San Francisco bay area nonprofit sector in a time of government retrenchment*. Washington, D.C.: Urban Institute Press, 1985.

Harvey, Philip D., & Snyder, James D. Charities need a bottom line too. *Harvard Business Review*, 1987, *65* (January–February), 14–22.

Hirsch, Paul M., & Davis, Harry L. Are arts administrators really serious about marketing? In Michael Mokwa & William Dawson (Eds.), *Marketing and the arts* (pp. 59–64). New York: Praeger, 1979.

Hobbes, Thomas. *Leviathan: On the matter, force and power of a commonwealth ecclesiastical and civil*. 1651.

Hodgkinson, Virginia Ann, & Weitzman, Murray S. *Dimensions of the independent sector: A statistical profile* (1st ed.). Washington, D.C.: Independent Sector, 1984.

———. *Dimensions of the independent sector: A statistical profile* (2nd ed.). Washington, D.C.: Independent Sector, 1986.

Hughes, Everett C. *The sociological eye: Selected papers*. New Brunswick, N.J.: Transaction, 1984.

Independent Sector. Organizing committee report. Washington, D.C.: Independent Sector, 1979.

Jaques, Elliott. Social analysis and the Glacier Project. In Elliott Jaques (Ed.), *Glacier Project Papers*. London: Heinemann Educational Books, 1965.

———. *A general theory of bureaucracy*. London: Heinemann Educational Books, 1976.

———. (Ed.). *Health services*. London: Heinemann Educational Books, 1978.

Keller, George. *Academic strategy: The management revolution in American higher education*. Baltimore: Johns Hopkins University Press, 1983.

Kovner, Anthony R. Improving the effectiveness of hospital governing boards. *Frontiers of Health Services Management*, 1985, (August), 4–33.

Kramer, Ralph M. The future of the voluntary agency in a mixed economy. *The Journal of Applied Behavioral Science*, 1985a, *21* (4), 377–391.

———. The voluntary agency in a mixed economy: Dilemmas of entrepreneurialism and vendorism. Working Paper No. 85, Program on Nonprofit Organizations, Institution for Social and Policy Studies, Yale University, 1985b.

Larson, Magali Sarfatti. *The rise of professionalism: A sociological analysis*. Berkeley: University of California Press, 1977.

Leavitt, Thomas W. The beleaguered director. In Brian O'Doherty (Ed.), *Museums in crisis* (pp. 91–102). New York: George Braziller, 1972.

Likert, Rensis. A motivation approach to the theory of organization. In Maison Haire (Ed.), *Modern organization theory* (pp. 184–217). New York: John Wiley & Sons, 1959.

Lippert, Paul G., Gutowski, M., & Salamon, Lester M. *The Atlanta nonprofit sector in a time of government retrenchment*. Washington, D.C.: Urban Institute Press, 1984.

McAdam, Terry W. *Careers in the nonprofit sector: Doing well by doing good*. Washington, D.C.: The Taft Group, 1986.

Majone, Giandomenico. Professionalism and nonprofit organizations. Working Paper No. 24, Program on Nonprofit Organizations, Institution for Social and Policy Studies, Yale University, October 1980.

Margulies, Rebecca Z., & Blau, Peter M. The pecking order of the elite: America's leading professional schools. *Change,* 1973, *5* (9, November), 21–27.

Mason, David E. *Voluntary nonprofit enterprise management.* New York: Plenum, 1984.

Mintzberg, Henry. *The nature of managerial work.* New York: Harper & Row, 1973.

Mirvis, Philip H., & Hackett, Edward J. Work and workforce characteristics in the nonprofit sector. *Monthly Labor Review,* 1983, *106* (April), 3–12.

Moynihan, Daniel P. Comments to the charter meeting of Independent Sector, 1979.

Neil, Gilbert. The commercialization of social welfare. *The Journal of Applied Behavioral Science,* 1985, *21* (4), 365–376.

Nielsen, Waldemar A. The third sector: Keystone of a caring society. Occasional paper. Washington, D.C.: Independent Sector, 1980.

O'Connell, Brian. *The board member's book.* New York: The Foundation Center, 1985.

————. *Effective leadership in voluntary organizations.* New York: Association Press, 1976.

Odendahl, Teresa Jean, Boris, Elizabeth Trocolli, & Daniels, Arlene Kaplan. *Working in foundations: Career patterns of women and men.* New York: The Foundation Center, 1985.

Patti, Rino J. *Social welfare administration: Managing social programs in a developmental context.* Englewood Cliffs, N.J.: Prentice-Hall, 1983.

Perrow, Charles. The analysis of goals in complex organizations. *American Sociological Review,* 1961, *26* (6), 854–866.

————. A framework for the comparative analysis of organizations. *American Sociological Review,* 1967, *32* (3), 194–208.

Peters, Thomas J., & Waterman, Robert H. Jr. *In search of excellence: Lessons from America's best-run companies.* New York: Harper & Row, 1982.

Peterson, Richard A. From impresario to arts administrator: Formal accountability in nonprofit cultural organizations. In Paul J. DiMaggio (Ed.), *Nonprofit enterprise in the arts: Studies in mission and constraint* (pp. 161–183). New York: Oxford University Press, 1986.

Pfeffer, Jeffrey, & Salancik, Gerald R. *The external control of organizations: A resource dependence perspective.* New York: Harper & Row, 1978.

Program on Nonprofit Organizations. *Research reports, 3.* Institution for Social and Policy Studies, Yale University, Fall 1984.

Reichert, Kurt. The drift toward entrepreneurialism in health and social welfare. *Administration in Social Work,* 1977, *1* (1, Summer), 171–181.

Reiss, Albert J., Jr. Occupational mobility of professional workers. *American Sociological Review,* 1955, *20* (6), 693–700.

Ritti, R. R., & Goldner, Fred H. Professional pluralism in an industrial organization. *Management Science,* 1969, *16* (4), B–233–B–246.

Rowbottom, Ralph. Professionals in health and social services organizations. In Elliott Jaques (Ed.), *Health Services.* London: Heinemann Educational Books, 1978.

————. & Billis, David. The stratification of work and organizational design. In Elliott Jaques (Ed.), *Health services.* London: Heinemann Educational Books, 1978.

Rudney, Gabriel, & Weitzman, Murray. Trends in employment and earnings in the philanthropic sector. *Monthly Labor Review*, 1984, *107* (9, September), 16–20.

Salamon, Lester M. *Partners in public service: Toward a theory of government-nonprofit relations*. Washington, D.C.: The Urban Institute, August 1985.

———., & Abramson, Alan J. *The federal budget and the nonprofit sector*. Washington, D.C.: Urban Institute Press, 1982.

Schein, Edgar H. *Organizational culture and leadership: A dynamic view*, San Francisco: Jossey-Bass, 1985.

Scott, W. Richard. Health care organizations in the 1980s: The convergence of public and professional control systems. In John W. Meyer & W. Richard Scott, *Organizational environments: Ritual and rationality* (pp. 99–127). Beverly Hills, Calif.: Sage Publications, 1983.

Selby, Cecily C. Better performance from "nonprofits." *Harvard Business Review*, 1978, *56* (September–October), 92–98.

Shestack, Alan. The director: Scholar and businessman, educator and lobbyist. *Museum News*, 1978, *57*, November–December, 27–31.

Simon, Herbert A. Theories of decision-making in economics and behavioral science. *American Economic Review*, 1959, *49* (3, June), 253–283.

Skloot, Edward. Enterprise and commerce in nonprofit organizations. In Walter W. Powell (Ed.), *The nonprofit sector: A research handbook* (pp. 380–393). New Haven: Yale University Press, 1987.

Stamp, Gillian. Assessment of individual capacity. In Elliott Jaques with R. O. Gibson, & D. J. Isaac (Eds.), *Levels of abstraction in logic and human action*. London: Heinemann Educational Books, 1978.

Unlocking the computer's profit potential. New York: McKinsey & Co., 1968.

Weber, Max. *The theory of social and economic organization* (A. M. Henderson & Talcott Parsons, trans.). New York: Oxford University Press, 1947.

Weil, Stephen. "Questioning Some Premises," *Museum News, 64*, No. 5, June 1986, pp. 20–27.

Wolf, Thomas. *The nonprofit organization: An operating manual*. Englewood Cliffs, N.J.: Prentice-Hall, 1984.

Young, Dennis R. *If not for profit, for what?: A behavioral theory of the nonprofit sector based on entrepreneurship*. Lexington, Mass.: Lexington Books, D. C. Heath & Co., 1983.

———. Performance and reward in nonprofit organizations: Evaluation, compensation, and personal incentives. Working paper No. 79, Program on Nonprofit Organizations, Institution for Social and Policy Studies, Yale University, January 1984.

———. What business can learn from nonprofits. Working paper, Nonprofit Management Education Project, W. Averell Harriman College, State University of New York at Stony Brook, November 1985.

Zolberg, Vera L. Tensions of mission in American art museums. In Paul J. DiMaggio (Ed.), *Nonprofit enterprise in the arts: Studies in mission and constraint* (pp. 184–198). New York: Oxford University Press, 1986.

Zucker, Lynne G. (Ed.). *Institutional theories of organizations: Culture and environment*. New York: Ballinger, 1986.

Index

Contributors

JONATHAN B. COOK is National Executive Director of the Support Centers of America, the nation's largest single provider of management assistance and consulting services to nonprofit organizations. He publishes the management sections of *The Nonprofit Times*. His publications include *Resources and Strategies for Improving the Management of Nonprofit Organizations*.

RICHARD M. CYERT is President of Carnegie-Mellon University and former Dean of the Graduate School of Industrial Administration at Carnegie-Mellon. His publications include *A Behavioral Theory of the Firm*, coauthored with James G. March, and *The Management of Nonprofit Organizations*.

ARLENE KAPLAN DANIELS is Professor, Department of Sociology, Northwestern University. Her publications include *Working in Foundations: Career Patterns of Women and Men*, coauthored with Teresa Odendahl and Elizabeth Boris, and the forthcoming *Invisible Careers: Women Civic Leaders in the Volunteer World*.

PAUL J. DiMAGGIO is Associate Professor, Institution for Social and Policy Studies, Sociology Department, and School of Organization and Management, Yale University, and Co-Chair of Yale's Program on Non-Profit Organizations. His publications include *Nonprofit Enterprise in the Arts: Studies in Mission and Constraint*.

MARK E. KEANE is Distinguished Visiting Professor of Public Administration and Association Management and Director of the Master's Degree Program in Association Management at George Washington University. He was an association executive from 1967 to 1983. He is Chairman of the Board of the National Academy of Public Administration.

ROBERT F. LEDUC is the founding President of the Institute for Nonprofit Organization Management in Denver, and was the founding Executive Director of the Technical Assistance Center in Denver, an organization providing management training and consulting service to nonprofit organizations. He is an adjunct faculty member of the Graduate School of Public Affairs at the University of Colorado at Denver.

REYNOLD LEVY is Corporate Vice President at AT&T and President of the AT&T Foundation. He was formerly the Executive Director of the 92nd Street Y in New York City, and has served as an adjunct faculty member at Baruch College of the City University of New York, New York University, Columbia University, Adelphi University, and the University of Missouri at Kansas City.

TERRY W. McADAM was, until his death in September 1986, Executive Vice President and Program Director of the Conrad N. Hilton Foundation. He was formerly Assistant Director and Senior Vice President of New York Community Trust. He was an adjunct faculty member at Fordham University, the New School for Social Research, New York University, and the University of San Francisco. His publications include *Careers in the Nonprofit Sector: Doing Well by Doing Good.*

ASTRID E. MERGET is Director and Professor, School of Public Administration, and Associate Dean, College of Business, Ohio State University. She was formerly Professor and Chair of the Department of Public Administration at George Washington University. She is past President of the National Association of Schools of Public Affairs and Administration.

BRIAN O'CONNELL is the founding President of Independent Sector, and was formerly National Director of the Mental Health Association. His publications include *Effective Leadership in Voluntary Organizations, America's Voluntary Spirit, The Board Member's Book,* and *Philanthropy in Action.*

MICHAEL O'NEILL is Professor and Director, Institute for Nonprofit Organization Management, College of Professional Studies, University of San Francisco. His publications include the forthcoming *The Third America: Private Nonprofit Organizations in the United States.*

SIMON SLAVIN is Adjunct Professor in the School of Social Work at Hunter College of the City University of New York, and Editor of the quarterly *Administration in Social Work*. He was the founding Dean of the School of Social Administration at Temple University.

BRUCE C. VLADECK is President of the United Hospital Fund of New York, and formerly Assistant Vice President of the Robert Wood Johnson Foundation and Assistant Commissioner for Health Planning and Resources Development in the New Jersey State Department of Health. He taught at Columbia University and has served on the adjunct faculty of Rutgers University, Princeton University, the College of Medicine and Dentistry of New Jersey, and New York University. His publications include *Unloving Care: The Nursing Home Tragedy*.

DENNIS R. YOUNG is Mandel Professor of Non-Profit Management and Director of the Mandel Center for Non-Profit Organizations, Case Western Reserve University. He was formerly Professor of Policy Analysis and Public Management and founding Director of Nonprofit Studies at the W. Averell Harriman College, State University of New York at Stony Brook. His publications include *If Not for Profit, for What?: A Behavioral Theory of the Nonprofit Sector Based on Entrepreneurship* and *Casebook of Management for Nonprofit Organizations*.

DATE DUE

DEMCO 38-297